THE FINANCIAL TSUNAMI

WILL IT DROWN US IN A WAVE OF DEBT?

MIKE GEARHARDT AND WILL GATES

www.TheFinancialTsunami.com

authorHOUSE®

AuthorHouse™
1663 Liberty Drive
Bloomington, IN 47403
www.authorhouse.com
Phone: 1-800-839-8640

First published by AuthorHouse 8/26/2010

ISBN: 978-1-4520-3912-1 (e)
ISBN: 978-1-4520-3909-1 (sc)
ISBN: 978-1-4520-3911-4 (hc)

Library of Congress Control Number: 2010910032

Printed in the United States of America
Bloomington, Indiana

This book is printed on acid-free paper.

FOREWORD

The mistake of many authors—as well as television and radio reporters and the editors and producers directing them—is misperceiving their readers, listeners, and viewers as possessing too little education, intelligence, or motivation to understand or to tolerate arguments expressed in more than a one-sentence quote or ten-second sound bite. As authors of *The Financial Tsunami*, Mike Gearhardt and Will Gates have made no such mistake about their readers. In fact, the absence of well-constructed and documented arguments in the media's coverage of the ongoing financial crisis led—if not compelled—the authors to write this book. For those of us who want to be convinced with evidence before making conclusions and who wish to arm ourselves with facts before entering a debate, this is the book.

Most refreshing about the authors' effort is the near absence of bias or political agenda. Conservatives and Liberals, Democrats and Republicans, moderates and extremists, Keynesians and Hayekists will likely find common ground in the authors' analysis of reckless government spending and their proposals for fiscally responsible solutions to America's financial mess.

Although extravagant governmental spending by Congress helps prove the authors' point that the government's largess must be reined in, no presidential administration in our lifetimes escapes their scrutiny. Even the Reagan administration is criticized for engaging in tax cuts and massive spending. While in part causing the collapse of the Soviet Union and reducing the threat of war with the Russians, they nonetheless set a pattern of government-unfunded spending that subsequent presidential administrations would follow. Yet as frightening as the deficit is now, the unfunded mandates of Social Security, Medicare, and the new health-care legislation will only exacerbate the problem.

The authors caution us not to be misled by government accounting tricks by which on-budget deficits are reduced by off-budget surpluses that hide the severity of the problem. We know that deficits are not merely a consequence of our government failing to collect enough taxes. There is a limit to the amount a minority of a society's citizens will pay to support a majority. Pointing to the will of the majority as a justification for the imposition of higher taxes is disingenuous. As George Bernard Shaw quipped, "A government which robs Peter to pay Paul can always depend on the support of Paul." Moreover, the American political system is based on not only the concept of majority rule but also a respect for minority rights.

The authors warn that we are not merely entering a financial crisis of the type we have encountered and survived before. Those of us who lived through the excesses of the 1960s and the stagnation of the 1970s and early 1980s and witnessed new levels of government spending, high interest rates, low economic growth, and high employment are easily misled to believe that just as Presidents Reagan and Clinton and the technological innovations of the 1980s and 1990s rescued the country from the malaise of the Carter administration, so too some new president, Congress, and entrepreneurial generation will perform another miracle to stave off financial ruin. To the contrary, the authors show that unless our government quickly reverses its financial course, the decades of the 2010s and beyond will see a financial collapse of unprecedented severity, breadth, and length. Greece's financial woes are a warning, they argue. But Greece is merely the financial equivalent of the state of Michigan, and if America slides over the brink of financial failure, there will not be a European Union, International Monetary Fund, or anyone else big enough to bail out the world's largest economy. Not even China.

So how do we Americans prevent the threat of a financial tsunami? The authors have a prescription that is as balanced and politically neutral as their criticisms, recognizing the need for both responsible spending and responsibility to ourselves and to our fellow citizens. While our present generations may not lose everything, we risk inflicting pain on our future generations as they foot the bill for the cost of government programs we defer to our children and our children's children. Yet there exist, the authors argue, appropriate levels of spending that meet our responsibilities.

We have to act now, however, and not let claims of expediency or inconvenience allow our politicians to drag their fiscally irresponsible feet. We should be reminded of the problem of inflation in the 1960s and 1970s. Today, the circumstances have changed, much to the worse, but the conclusion is the same: America's huge financial deficits are everyone's problem.

Dr. Thomas Bowers
Commercial & Corporate Finance Law
Department of Business Law & Ethics
Kelley Graduate School of Business
Indiana University-Bloomington

TABLE OF CONTENTS

Introduction 1

The Financial Tsunami 3
We need to act before it's too late!

Fuzzy Math 9
Is it fuzzy or deceptive?

Fiscal Responsibility 15
What does it look like?

Fiscal Responsibility Has Disappeared 21
Where did it go?

Recessions Are Inevitable 27
They will happen again and again and again.

Affordable Housing and the Housing Crisis 33
A failed government mandate

Cash for Clunkers 39
Was the money well spent?

The Evolution of Taxes 43
*Do higher taxes lead to government expansion,
or does government expansion lead to higher taxes?*

Sources of Revenue 47
Is there really a money tree?

Who Pays and How Much 51
If 47 million filers didn't pay any taxes in 2007, then who did?

Taxes and the Deficit..57
Will increasing taxes eliminate the deficit?

Outlays and Their Impact on the National Debt 63
The government loves to spend our money.

A Need for Balance and Priority.................................69
Have we failed to invest, or have we just spent unwisely?

On-Budget/Off-Budget Deficits and Surpluses.............73
Now you see it; now you don't.

Intergovernmental Debt is Really Public Debt..............77
You can ignore it, but it is not going away.

Where Does the Money Go? 85
Our nation has a spending problem!

Social Security Trust Fund 91
The good news is that the SSTF has $2.7 trillion.
The bad news is it is invested in government IOUs.

Medicare 97
It is in very poor health.
Don't call the doctor, because we can't afford one.

It's Time to Sink or Swim..103
We have the ability to stay afloat,
but it will require change and sacrifice.

Appendixes...113

Notes 121

INTRODUCTION

The U.S. economy is in deep trouble and shows no sign of improving anytime soon. What's different today from yesterday, five years ago, or ten years ago? Why are those things different? These are fair questions, and they will be examined.

For starters, our nation has never:

➢ Had a $2 trillion annual deficit
➢ Had a $13 trillion national debt
➢ Had an unfunded Social Security actuarial liability of $7 trillion
➢ Had an unfunded Medicare actuarial liability of $36 trillion
➢ Projected an average annual deficit of $850 billion for the next ten years
➢ Projected a national debt of $25 trillion in the next ten years
➢ Projected to have a national debt that exceeds the GDP of the nation for an extended period

These are serious numbers. They are even more serious given the fact that the U.S. government takes in only $2.7 trillion in revenue per year. Solving these problems is going to take a lot of money and reductions in some federally sponsored programs. The money will ultimately be paid by the citizens of this country. Knowing how that money can be generated and understanding why some programs must be cut will help in getting the economy back on course.

Financial responsibility will be a recurring theme throughout this book. While financial responsibility is important, it needs to be tempered with social responsibility. The problem we face is that those who are advocates of social responsibility and those who advocate financial responsibility have differing mind-sets that preclude them from hearing and understanding the others' messages. To mitigate the coming tax and program changes, both sides must understand that there will need to be painful sacrifices made to save our economy. Reading newspapers or business periodicals, watching any of the omnipresent news channels, or just talking to friends should be enough to make anyone aware that the United States of America has an economic problem. Typical coverage of the deficit and other economic issues by the mass media makes it clear that the economy is ailing, but the mass media fails to offer realistic assessments of the magnitude of the problem. That may be because many sources of information choose to present "news" in a way that sells advertising and downplays the issues that are not as salable. Our financial problems are very serious. They cannot be glossed over. Americans need to know the consequences of our government's fiscal irresponsibility.

While some analysts attempt to draw parallels between historical economic trends and the current state of the economy, their analysis fails to recognize the situational differences. Our economy is in uncharted waters. The current state of the U.S. economy is unlike any other in our nation's history. Attempting to draw parallels only serves to confuse and understate the problem. It draws a false conclusion based on historical data that is simply not relevant.

The fact that you picked up this book indicates that you have an interest in the nation's current economic situation. Understanding the impact that the federal budget has on our quality of life and the economy is necessary if we plan on involving ourselves in the political process that will shape the nation's future. The nation's finances are fast approaching the breaking point.

THE FINANCIAL TSUNAMI
WE NEED TO ACT BEFORE IT'S TOO LATE!

The following chart illustrates that national debt was practically nonexistent prior to 1970. In 2010, it is projected to be $13,786,615,000,000. In five years, it is expected to increase by 43 percent, to almost $20 trillion.

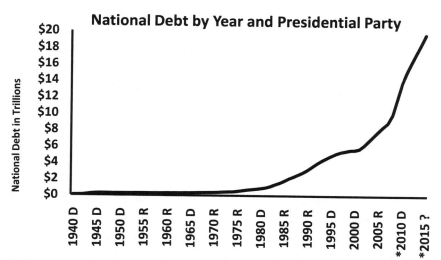

* Estimate   Table 7.1—Federal Debt at the End of Year: 1940–2015
http://www.whitehouse.gov/omb/budget/Historicals/

Decades of fiscal irresponsibility due to excessive spending, inconsistent and irrational tax policies, growth in entitlement programs, government intervention into free markets, and inadequate accounting practices threaten to drown our nation's economy under a wave of debt. While the government has failed to take any meaningful actions to address our mounting debt, the magnitude of the problem has been recognized by the U.S. Government Accountability Office (GAO). The following quote from GAO document GAO-09-405SP, Long-Term Fiscal Outlook March 2009, references long-term simulations that show:

> Absent policy actions aimed at reforming the key drivers of our structural deficits—health care spending and social security—the federal government faces unsustainable growth in debt. The longer that action to deal with the federal government's long-term fiscal outlook is delayed, the greater the risk that the eventual changes will be disruptive and destabilizing.

"Disruptive and destabilizing"—how much stronger can the statement be? In addition to alerting us to the potential risk, they also identified the key drivers of the problem as health care and Social Security spending. This is not some historical quote taken out of context; it is both current and relevant and is unfortunately being ignored. Certainly no government agency would make such an alarming statement if they did not believe it to be true. This is not a lone department making this comment. Similar comments have been made by other agencies and in other Trustees Reports, including the Social Security Trustees Report. It is unimaginable that more attention isn't being directed toward these issues.

The wave of debt can be as intimidating as the thousands of line items in the federal budget and the amount of dollars the government is forecasting that it will spend. Gaining a basic understanding of the budget process and government accounting is an arduous task. While the full budget detail may be interesting, the simple fact is that Social Security, Medicare and Medicaid, net interest, and defense spending typically account for approximately 65 percent of all federal spending. These four accounts are the focus of this book, as they represent the greatest risk to the future of the nation's economy. An understanding of the current and future spending in these accounts, along with knowledge of government accounting practices and tax policy, is necessary to comprehend just how ominous the nation's financial outlook really is.

2009 Ranking of National Debt—Top Ten Countries

Country	National Debt
United States	$13,450,000,000,000
United Kingdom	$9,088,000,000,000
Germany	$5,208,000,000,000
France	$5,021,000,000,000
Netherlands	$3,733,000,000,000
Spain	$2,410,000,000,000
Italy	$2,403,500,000,000
Ireland	$2,287,000,000,000
Japan	$2,132,000,000,000
Luxembourg	$1,994,000,000,000

Since the late 1960s, the United States has been a global leader in fiscal irresponsibility as national debt grew from billions to hundreds of billions. In 1982, a new era of debt was ushered in as we crossed the trillion-dollar debt threshold for the first time. In 1986, only four years later, our national debt surpassed the $2 trillion mark. By 1992 it had exceeded $4 trillion; in 2006 it had grown to $8 trillion; and today it is in excess of $13 trillion.

It doesn't stop there. According to President Obama's 2011 budget, released in February 2010, the national debt is expected to be $24.4 trillion by 2019. As a point of reference, the 2010 budget projected the national debt would be $23.1 trillion by 2019. In one year, the debt projection for 2019 grew a whopping $1.3 trillion. This shows the shortcomings of governmental forecasting and just how dramatically the numbers can change.

If the president's estimates prove to be correct, sometime between 2011 and 2012 the size of the federal debt will be greater than the estimated U.S. Gross Domestic Product (GDP). This means that our debt will be greater than the total market value of all goods and services produced in our country in that year. Looking at this from a different perspective, the debt of the United States will approximate the combined GDP of the next three largest economies in the world (China, Japan, and India).

Why should we be concerned now? What's so different today from yesterday? Plenty! This financial tsunami has been growing for decades but has thus far been ignored. Metaphorically, we have been standing on the beach unconcerned because we can't see the gigantic wave of debt about to inundate us, but unquestionably, it is coming.

There are many reasons why we can no longer ignore this financial tsunami. For starters, the debt numbers continue to grow with no end in sight, as evidenced by the president's 2011 budget and Congress's recent increase of the debt ceiling. Another reason for concern is that the government continues to intervene in free-market activities, which have in turn contributed to disruptions and fluctuations in the economy. Bailouts, incentives for consumers, and policy changes are several ways that the government has chosen to intervene in free-market activities. It is not unusual that when problems in free markets arise they are attributed to greed and the opportunity is seized to bash the free-enterprise system. Criticizing banks for causing the housing and subprime crisis was convenient. But the facts show that the government's policies and actions played a significant role and ultimately fueled the collapse of the housing market.

Continuing and growing deficits are another concern. The maturing of Social Security, Lyndon Johnson's Great Society, and years of Ronald Reagan's tax cuts have resulted in our nation borrowing money to fund annual budget deficits. It's similar to paying a home mortgage with a credit card. Incurring additional debt to pay debt just doesn't make sense and only defers the problem.

For most of our nation's history, we experienced budget surpluses. But those days are gone. This growing wave of debt has been building for forty years. Our nation currently projects and budgets for deficits each and every year for at least the next ten years. The ten-year period does not necessarily represent the end of the cycle. It merely represents the duration of the government forecast period. Current government agency reports would indicate that this problem will exist well beyond the ten-year forecast period and may exist for several more decades. The deficits are not funding an economic crisis or war, although these are certainly contributors, but instead are funding programs that artificially support our standard of living. We cannot remain a world leader if we continue on this reckless path.

At the current $13 trillion level, the U.S. national debt equates to $42,000 for every citizen in the country—not every taxpayer, but every citizen. This means that every child born in the United States at the time this book was written was born with $42,000 of debt. No wonder they issue Social Security numbers to infants.

In addition to the $13.8 trillion of national debt, the nation has amassed an unfunded liability that amounts to approximately $70 trillion. This unfunded liability represents the future benefits for Social Security and Medicare. The corresponding projected funding to support these benefits is inadequate to meet the outlays. The difference between the two is the unfunded liability. Why don't we hear more about this? It has to do with the inadequate accounting practices used by the U.S. government.

No one will knock on your door to collect the debt, but it is taxpayer debt that is in the form of U.S. Treasury obligations. We are all going to have to pay the debt with taxes at some point. As a nation, we can't continue to borrow indefinitely, and the magnitude of these numbers should absolutely terrify every citizen of this nation. The continued growth of national debt will encumber future generations, leaving our children and grandchildren to pay for the tremendous financial burden that we have created in less than forty years.

Why is the debt continuing to grow? The reasons are many. Entitlement programs, such as Social Security, Medicaid, and Medicare, that perpetuate increases in spending are just beginning to come of age and will cause outlays to soar in coming years. Many of the programs, in particular Social Security and Medicare, were initiated to provide a safety net for an aging population. As baby boomers access these programs, participation will grow from current levels of fifty-one million to seventy-seven million by 2025, which is more than a 50 percent increase in participation. Many other programs (i.e., Medicare Part D, the subsidized prescription drug program) have been implemented and expanded during periods of rapid economic growth under the assumption that the growth would continue indefinitely. As the debt escalates, the government will have to increase taxes, borrow more, and/or cut spending.

Although future revenue increases will be necessary, caution must be taken to avoid suppressing economic growth. Relying on taxes alone will have a negative effect on economic growth. Increases in taxes reduce the funds available for investment, and reduced investment results in fewer jobs being created. Fewer jobs result in reduced tax revenue, and the government once again will have to increase taxes to generate the same level of revenue. There is only so much money available in an economy. The more the government takes out via taxes, the less there is for investment and, by extension, jobs.

While taxes and spending ran amuck, an inadequate accounting system failed to track the growing liabilities associated with future outlays. The federal government uses a cash accounting system, which is essentially a "pay as you go" system and does not account for known future and past liabilities until they are paid. As a result, liabilities continue to grow with little or no recognition. Under the "pay as you go" system, by the time unfunded growth is recognized, it is already out of control. It is the growth in these unfunded future liabilities, similar to a giant earthquake at the floor of the ocean, that will amplify the financial tsunami. An example of the magnitude of unfunded liabilities is found in the 2009 Board of Trustees of the Federal Hospital Insurance and Federal Supplementary Medical Insurance Trust Funds Report (HI), wherein the board acknowledges that the fund has an estimated unfunded obligation of $36.4 trillion. The report states, "In other words, increases in revenues and/or reductions in benefit expenditures—equivalent to a lump-sum amount today of more than $13 trillion—would be required to bring the HI trust fund into long-range financial balance." It continues, "Extending the calculations beyond 2083 adds $23.0 trillion in unfunded obligations to the amount estimated through 2083."

The problem is growing. The longer we wait to take action, the more drastic the actions will have to be.

FUZZY MATH

IS IT FUZZY OR DECEPTIVE?

Many found the "fuzzy math" reference by presidential candidate George W. Bush in 2000 to be somewhat humorous and shrugged it off, assuming that he was just avoiding a question or being inept. Some believed that he did not have a firm grasp of the issues and chose to jokingly sidestep the question. As we have come to learn, his reference was more truthful than humorous as he saw the problem for what it was. Today, the United States is experiencing "fuzzy math" that can no longer be joked about and ignored. In the face of continuing record deficits, admonishments from trading partners about the magnitude of our nation's debt, high unemployment, and crises in banking, manufacturing, real estate, and elsewhere, the time has come to remove the haze from around the "fuzzy math" and understand what is behind the numbers.

Many of us are functionally illiterate when it comes to understanding the federal government's budget numbers, which range in the trillions of dollars. "Fuzzy math" is the result of this lack of understanding and/or apathy about the financial condition of our nation. Let's look at an example that will help put the federal debt into some perspective.

Suppose you have an insatiable appetite to spend and want to go on a shopping spree with the objective of spending $1,000 per minute. How long would it take to spend the current federal debt of $13,800,000,000,000?

Spending per minute	$1,000
Dollars spent per hour	$60,000
Dollars spent per day	$1,440,000
Dollars spent per year	$525,600,000
$13.8 trillion divided by $525.6 million	26,255 years

As the numbers show, it would take 26,255 years to spend the federal debt. That would be quite a shopping spree both in size and duration.

Citizens are not the only ones who need a better understanding of the budget math. It would appear that many of those elected to Congress and other public offices also need to be better educated in the area of budget math and numbers in general. Go to YouTube and listen to Nancy Pelosi's stimulus package speech. On January 24, 2009, prior to passage of the package, she stated, "Every month we don't pass this package, 500 million will lose their jobs."

Talk about not understanding the numbers. There are only 310 million people in the United States, and about 45 percent of those are in the workforce, which means the U.S. workforce in totality is approximately 140 million people. This comment was made by the Speaker of the House, the third-highest elected office in our nation, and was aired on all the networks and thus became a source of "fact" for many. This simple misstated fact was repeated in the news, online, and in conversations. The problem is that such misstatements, if left uncorrected, become facts by default. Often it is these "facts" that are used by those who support or oppose an issue. We accept them as facts since we are hearing them from supposedly reliable sources. While the Speaker's supporters were quick to note that her statement was a mathematical slipup, it was never actually corrected.

If we want to have a strong nation that is recognized as a world leader and capable of protecting and providing for its citizens, our country must learn to live within its means. Programs shouldn't be created or endorsed unless it can be shown that they can be funded. If we can't afford a program, it should be modified or discontinued. Americans need to identify and rally around a systematic long-term plan that will allow our nation to rid itself of the mounting deficits that threaten the way of life for both current and future generations. If we fall into the same short-term thinking as the people of Greece, whose citizens have rioted, burned buildings, called strikes, and protested over increases in taxes and spending reductions, we will have missed the opportunity to persuade our leaders to develop meaningful solutions to our mounting economic problems. Our nation would then suffer a fate similar to other economically irresponsible countries that have failed to develop solutions to remedy their problems. Our nation's creditors will dictate the levels of our spending and taxes just as the European Union (EU) is now dictating the future of Greece's. We would then no longer be an independent and free nation.

It makes no difference if you are an Independent, Democrat, or Republican; every citizen should be outraged at the financial condition of our country. Many of the financial problems our country faces are attributed to a lack of regulation and/or greed. While these may be contributing factors, it has been our leaders, regardless of party, who have failed to make the hard decisions and reform the programs that are jeopardizing our future. If these leaders refuse to take steps to address the financial problems our nation faces, then they need to be held accountable by the voters.

Discussions on abortion, the right to bear arms, global warming, and many other topics are distractions used to divert the focus from the issue of the economic health of our nation. In today's financial environment, we all are more aware of our individual income and debt. Over the last twenty-four months, we all have witnessed the consequences of someone taking on more debt than they can afford. While many of us have tightened our budgets and are watching our spending, the government continues to increase the national debt to unprecedented levels. Why shouldn't our government show the same sense of fiscal responsibility as many of us have?

The size of the deficit is not a party problem. It is a political problem, and history clearly shows that both parties are capable of reckless spending. This is evidenced by the fact that the United States has not experienced a decline in the national debt since 1969. This includes the "fuzzy math" of the Clinton era's surplus, which we will see later in this book in a case study on "fuzzy math." The deficit has grown under both Republicans and Democrats, and neither party has shown a willingness to work with the other to develop a model that deals with balancing the budget and reducing the federal debt.

As the following chart shows, the deficit was near zero from 1940 to 1970. Since then our nation has run a deficit, which is now nearly $2 trillion a year.

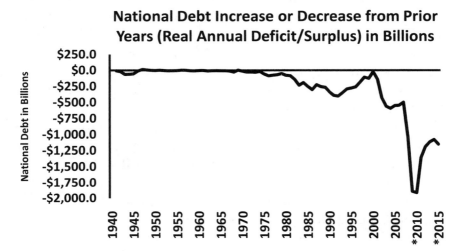

National Debt Increase or Decrease from Prior Years (Real Annual Deficit/Surplus) in Billions

*Estimate   Table 1.1 and 7.1 OMB Historical Tables 2011
http://www.whitehouse.gov/omb/budget/Historicals/

We have experienced recessions in the past, and spending our way out of a recession has resulted in escalating debt levels. Taxing and spending is not a solution for correcting a fiscal crisis. The "tax and spend" philosophy has historically resulted in a continued expansion of the national debt. In fact, since 1940 we have had only five years where the national debt did not increase. National debt has increased in seventy-four out of the last seventy-nine years. While advocating tax increases on the wealthy (however wealthy is defined) makes for good press, it is a mathematical impossibility to increase taxes on the wealthy high enough to significantly address a $13.8 trillion national debt.

While fiscal facts are not that hard to come by, they are often not sought, found, or heeded. An understanding of the facts is necessary to challenge and understand the inconsistencies of our nation's finances. As a nation, we have implemented programs that are not sustainable in their current form. Government agencies such as the Congressional

Budget Office (CBO) and Office of Management and Budget (OMB) recognize the problem, but their hands are often tied by politics.

Draw your own conclusions about what is needed to leave a viable economy for future generations, but do so understanding the facts by looking at available information. Twenty years ago, with limited access to information, we had to have some level of belief in what we were told. Today, with the technology at hand, citizens can access the facts and research the issues. If we don't become informed voters soon, the American dream will become something that is read about in history books, perhaps written in Chinese.

It is time to peel back the fuzz and get at the facts.

FISCAL RESPONSIBILITY
WHAT DOES IT LOOK LIKE?

The following graph shows the total federal government receipts and outlays. The widening gap between the lines illustrates the trend toward excessive government spending.

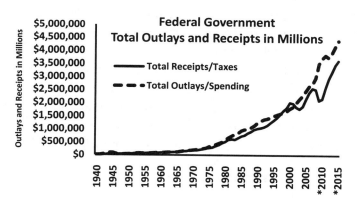

* Estimate   Table 1.1—Summary of Receipts, Outlays, and Surplusses or Deficits (-) 1940-2015
http://www.whitehouse.gov/omb/budget/Historicals/

The lines from 1940 to 1982 are what government fiscal responsibility looked like. The graph shows that over a period of forty years, the government, regardless of party, managed to match spending and outlays very closely. The lack of debt and the resulting stability are the reasons that the U.S. dollar became the standard currency for global trade. Since that time, spending has exceeded revenues, sending us on a steady march toward fiscal irresponsibility. Even though the chart shows that revenue exceeded outlays in early 2000, this is due to government accounting and does not reflect reality. Since figures are based on government data, the numbers tend to be more politically motivated than substantive. The accounting associated with the year 2000 numbers will be discussed later. The fact is that the national debt has increased every year since 1969.

Fiscal responsibility is an elusive concept that many administrations over the past forty years, with the possible exception of President Clinton, have not demonstrated an ability to address. During his presidency, Clinton was successful in driving the nation toward a balanced budget. Since his tenure was not that long ago, maybe there is a lesson to be learned about fiscal responsibility.

We are all more cognizant of our financial health today than we were just a short time ago. What changed? As former president Clinton so aptly put it in his first campaign, "It's the economy, stupid." Unemployment, underemployment, growing debt, and little if any savings have made us all acutely aware of our finances. A few years ago, many citizens, believing that the economic boom would last forever, jumped into the housing market. They paid inflated prices and assumed excessive or unmanageable debt. The result was a staggering increase in defaults and personal bankruptcies. Many learned that excess spending will lead to financial disaster. If our government continues to ignore the need for fiscal responsibility, specifically balancing revenues and outlays, it will experience a similar fate. The failure to manage spending increases an already out-of-control debt and quickens our date with financial disaster.

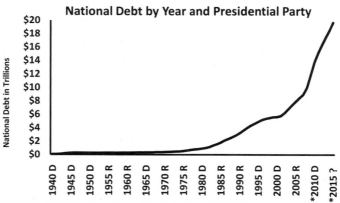

* Estimate   Table 7.1—Federal Debt at the End of Year: 1940–2015
http://www.whitehouse.gov/omb/budget/Historicals/

Fiscal responsibility has less to do with the size of government and more to do with the effectiveness of government. Effectiveness means working within the confines of the revenue collected and allocating those revenues in the most efficient way possible to benefit the population as a whole. Fiscal responsibility may mean that the country will not be able to support all programs that citizens and politicians, collectively or individually, believe are worthy. Fiscal responsibility will not insure that the nation will have a budget surplus every year, but it does recognize the fact that a balanced budget and controlled spending is desirable and necessary over time. While developing a definition of fiscal responsibility that everyone can agree on is unlikely, at a minimum the definition should include:

> Recognizing an economic problem, identifying the size of the problem, and taking the necessary actions to address the problem

> Identifying the future costs of the existing programs and determining how to fund future obligations and/or determining what will need to be eliminated or cut back to make programs such as Social Security and Medicare viable for future generations

The recognition of the need for sound fiscal controls, identifying economic problems and associated costs and dealing with realistic numbers, is evidenced by the twenty-seven nations in the European Union. They adopted the Maastricht Treaty and established an annual deficit limit of no greater than 3 percent of GDP. Having twenty-seven nations that have not been politically aligned over the course of history agree on anything signifies the importance of the treaty. The treaty recognized that deficits may be higher during periods of temporary circumstances but established the 3 percent benchmark as a long-term standard. If the European Union, with its diverse cultures and economies, can identify and recognize the potential risk of not exercising fiscal control, it would seem that our nation should be capable of doing the same. A deficit no greater than 3 percent of GDP may not be the right number for all nations, but at least the European Union has an established target.

Politicians like to pontificate about fiscal responsibility. It is most often discussed during elections in abstract terms broad enough to avoid accountability. The time has come for the abstract to become concrete. This will give voters the ability to track the fiscal responsibility of politicians. Fiscal responsibility can take on different forms depending on circumstances. While some cite the Reagan tax cuts as evidence that lower taxes prompt economic growth, others can point to the economic growth and reduction in national debt that occurred after Clinton increased taxes. The fact is that both arguments are correct, because economic expansion or contraction is dependent on many factors other than just taxes. For example, technological advances during the Clinton era resulted in an increase in capital spending. That spending by both corporations and individuals, in an effort to keep pace with technology, resulted in an expansion of the economy. Economics is *not* an exact science. When chemists add chemicals together, they have a high degree of certainty of the outcome; however, when economists look at history and relationships to predict outcomes, the number of current variables and/or the relationship between the historical variables in economic models means that the models are not predictable with a high degree of certainty.

President Obama recognized the need for responsibility and titled his first budget a "New Era of Responsibility." Unfortunately, he completely omitted the word *fiscal*. In his 2011 budget, he is clear that fiscal responsibility is of utmost importance as evidenced by his desire to establish a bipartisan fiscal commission charged with identifying additional policies to put our country on a fiscally sustainable path of balancing the budget by 2015. His goal for a balanced budget excludes interest payments on the debt. Today our nation is experiencing the worst financial crisis since the Great Depression. Our leaders are pushing programs that will only exacerbate the problem. Is it responsible to advocate the promotion of socially responsible programs like healthcare reform or cap-and-trade legislation as major objectives while the American worker remains unemployed? Those advocating socially responsible programs must realize that without adequate funding those programs will fail and/or become a drag on the economy.

The top priority of government right now should be to stimulate the economy, create jobs, and address the issues that are suppressing economic growth. Our nation should not be rushing to create more programs when the financial impact cannot be determined with any degree of certainty. If we are not successful at creating jobs and thus creating the tax revenue that goes along with them, we will not be able to continue to support current programs without causing an inflationary cycle that could potentially bring down our entire economic system. Implementing new programs that require more government spending will only accelerate the demise of the current programs. If we leave future generations with a financial burden that cannot be supported, the opportunities that our society has enjoyed for generations will vanish. This loss will be viewed as a failure of our generation regardless of how successful the new programs are deemed. Often, well-intentioned programs are put in place without the knowledge of where future funding will originate. Is it responsible to leave a legacy of debt to our children because our current leaders could not make the tough decisions to drive our nation toward a balance of social and fiscal responsibility?

It is difficult to tell what fiscal responsibility looks like, as many of us have not been alive long enough to have experienced it.

FISCAL RESPONSIBILITY HAS DISAPPEARED
WHERE DID IT GO?

Prior to the '80s, our nation had embarked on a thirty-five-year journey toward fiscal responsibility. From 1946 to 1981, our national debt decreased from 121 percent of GDP to 32 percent of GDP, its lowest level since the great depression. From 1981 to 2009, we have seen national debt climb to over 70 percent of GDP, and it is still climbing. The 2011 budget projects that the national debt will exceed GDP in government fiscal year (GFY) 2013. (The government uses a fiscal year from October 1 to September 30 instead of the traditional calendar year.)

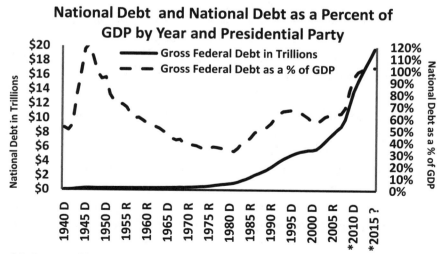

National Debt and National Debt as a Percent of GDP by Year and Presidential Party

* Estimate   Table 7.1—Federal Debt at the End of Year: 1940–2015
http://www.whitehouse.gov/omb/budget/Historicals/

The preceding graph shows the dollar value of the national debt and the national debt as a percent of GDP by presidential party at the beginning of each term. When Republicans occupied the White House, the debt increased substantially faster (in some cases twice as fast) than when Democrats occupied the White House. This fact has less to do with the party in office and more to do with the fact that cuts in taxes and/or increases in spending results in increased debt.

The graph illustrates that national debt declined from 121 percent to 32 percent of GDP during the period between President Truman and President Carter. Even though debt as a percent of GDP was declining, debt in absolute dollar terms did not decline, and in fact the dollar value of debt outstanding has increased every year since 1969. (We will discuss the apparent dip in the early 2000s elsewhere in the book.) During this period, between Truman and Carter, there were three Republican and three Democratic administrations (Kennedy and Johnson are counted as one administration), so both parties can lay claim to the reduction in the national debt as a percent of GDP during this period. Unquestionably the nation was moving in an economically positive direction, and the standard of living of many Americans improved. Since President Carter's tenure, however, the percent of national debt to GDP has moved rapidly higher, and the standard of living for all Americans will ultimately be adversely affected.

During the Reagan presidency, national debt climbed from 32 percent to 49 percent of GDP. Revenues grew by 65 percent and outlays grew by 69 percent, which is an obvious recipe for debt. Reagan's tax cuts, the largest in modern times, jump-started the economy but were *not* accompanied by spending cuts, and the net result was that national debt increased from $998 billion to $2.6 trillion, an increase of 161 percent. Many believe this to be the origin of our current national debt crisis. Based on the national debt numbers, it's hard to refute that point. While it may be argued that the tax cuts made during Reagan's term were irresponsible, the nation's GDP grew by a whopping 88 percent during his presidency.

Mandatory spending during Reagan's terms increased by $184 billion, or 61 percent, including spending on Medicare, Medicaid, and Social Security (defined as mandatory entitlement programs), which escalated from $196 billion to $358 billion—an increase of 83 percent.

This means that 88 percent of the increase in mandatory spending was attributable to increases in the costs of the programs that were implemented decades earlier. The numbers do not reflect the fact that the increase in entitlement spending is not yet being driven by the influx of the baby-boomer generation. As the following charts indicate, when baby boomers start participating in these programs, the outlays will escalate dramatically. The over-sixty-five population will have doubled from 2000 to 2030. In half that time, the combination of Social Security, Medicare, and Medicaid outlays will have tripled. President Obama's 2011 budget does not project social insurance outlays beyond 2015, but the trend is obvious and frightening. This demonstrates the risk of creating programs using politically motivated economic assumptions that result in inaccurate projections of future costs without identifying the source of future funding.

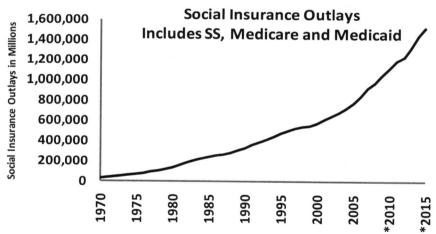

* Estimate Table 13.1—CASH INCOME, OUTGO, AND BALANCES OF
THE SOCIAL SECURITY AND MEDICARE TRUST FUNDS: 1970–2015
http://www.gpoaccess.gov/usbudget/fy11/hist.html

Reagan also increased defense spending in the '80s, which resulted in a cold-war peace dividend that allowed defense spending during the Clinton presidency to be reduced by an estimated $800 billion.

During the term of G. H. Bush, the forty-first president, GDP grew 13 percent. During his time in office, national debt grew from 49 percent to 66 percent of GDP. National debt in dollars increased

54 percent, growing to $4.4 trillion. During this period, mandatory spending also increased by 38 percent. To his credit, and at the peril of his reelection hopes, President Bush reversed his campaign promise and did recognize the need to increase taxes in order to address the burgeoning national debt.

President Clinton presided over a GDP expansion of 52 percent. During his two terms in office, tax revenues increased by 72 percent. The national debt declined from 66 percent to 57 percent of GDP. However, the national debt in dollars increased by 32 percent, growing from $4.3 trillion to $5.8 trillion. Mandatory programs continued their upward spiral, increasing by 53 percent during his eight years in office.

G. W. Bush, the forty-third president, saw the GDP grow by 40 percent during his presidency to slightly over $14 trillion. His terms saw national debt as a percent of GDP escalate from 57 percent to 83 percent of GDP, and the national debt swelled to $11.8 trillion. During this same period, entitlement spending increased by 70 percent.

From President Reagan to President G. W. Bush, the nation's GDP grew from $2.7 trillion to slightly more than $14 trillion. This was significant growth by any measure. During this same period national debt grew from less than $1 trillion to nearly $12 trillion. Today, the rate of growth of government spending is twice the rate of GDP growth. The reality is that the traditional economic measurements of prosperity, such as job creation, unemployment, interest rate levels, and housing starts, lose their relevance if the government spending rate continues to exceed the growth rate of the GDP.

The facts show that neither party has demonstrated an ability or willingness to exercise fiscal responsibility. The unwillingness to work together for the good of the nation is supported by an analysis of the party in control of the White House, Senate, and House. From 1987 to 1993, when Democrats were in charge of both the Senate and House and Republicans controlled the White House, the national debt increased by $2 trillion. From 1995 to 1999, while Democrats controlled the White House and Republicans controlled the Senate and House, the national deficit increased by $600 billion. From 2003 to 2005 Republicans controlled all three offices and the national deficit increased by $1.2 trillion. While both parties advocate fiscal responsibility, there is no evidence of it in reality.

The fuzzy math we discussed earlier sometimes distorts reality and produces unexpected results. In December 2003, President Bush signed the Medicare Part D program designed to assist older citizens in paying for prescription drugs. Many felt that the legislation was irresponsible from its inception, but neither party was willing to sacrifice votes for fiscal responsibility, so the Part D bill became law. What was irresponsible about the legislation? In 2003 it was estimated that Medicare Part D would cost taxpayers approximately $400 billion over a ten-year period. In 2006, just three years later, it was estimated that the plan would cost $725 billion over the same ten-year period. On a positive note, a survey by ABC News indicated that 65 percent of the enrollees were satisfied with the program. They should be satisfied, as they are getting a significant benefit at the expense of the American taxpayers.

Many rationalized that Medicare Part D was no more irresponsible or costly than other programs passed into law. There is a bit of irony in politicians touting fiscal responsibility while they vote along party lines on bills that advance an agenda that lack fiscal controls. An example of this behavior is when then-congressman Obama led a Democratic effort to defeat a Social Security restructuring bill. The Democratic Party celebrated their victory over the Republicans. President Obama's own Treasury Secretary, Tim Geithner, in his role as managing trustee of Social Security and Medicare programs, issued the following conclusion on Social Security in the 2009 Annual Trustees Report:

> The financial difficulties facing Social Security and Medicare pose serious challenges. For Social Security, the reform options are relatively well understood but the choices are difficult. Medicare is a bigger challenge. Its cost growth can be contained without sacrificing quality of care only if health-care cost growth more generally is contained. But despite the difficulties— indeed, because of the difficulties—it is essential that action be taken soon, particularly to control health-care costs.

The defeat created a false sense of victory. We realize now that there was nothing to celebrate. It was more of the same politics we have seen for years; the same politics that are still overshadowing our legislatures.

That leads to the question, where is *your* fiscal responsibility? Is it all about today and what is good for you *now*? Achieving fiscal responsibility is going to take sacrifice. Past generations gave their lives to preserve the freedoms we enjoy, while our sacrifice will only be financial. Our financial sacrifice will give our children and their children an opportunity to achieve the same quality of life we currently enjoy.

Fiscal responsibility cannot remain missing for much longer.

RECESSIONS ARE INEVITABLE
THEY WILL HAPPEN AGAIN AND AGAIN AND AGAIN.

The mention of the word *recession* brings either fear or joy to the heart of a politician. The politician in office will be vilified. The one seeking office has the opportunity to look intelligent by making bold statements of the obvious. In a society that loves to assign blame to almost everything, a recession often results in the incumbent party member being voted out of office. The fact is that, in a capitalistic society, recessions and even depressions are inevitable. They have occurred in the past, they are going to happen in the future, and there is little anyone can do to change that. Recessions and depressions are seldom the fault of a specific political party or administration but are often the culmination of actions that were taken in prior years.

While the blame game for the current recession is rampant in Washington, history shows that the events that typically lead to a recession are the result of dynamic shifts in market conditions, changes in general economic conditions, or changes in governmental policy. Policy changes can impact both free-market dynamics and consumer spending habits. The impact of many governmental actions and programs is often not realized for many years, in some cases decades, thus making it easier to distort the facts and reasons behind the recessional problem.

We are going to examine a few of the root causes of the current recession to show they are not just the result of greed and stupidity by banks, bankers, real-estate developers, or investment managers. In fact, the current recession can largely be tied to political actions taken fifteen years earlier. Many of the politicians who initiated programs that caused our current financial problems are still in office today.

Since the Great Depression, there have been twelve recessions according to the National Bureau of Economic Research (NBER). The inception date, duration, consensus cause for the recession, and the party occupying the White House are indicated in the following chart.

Year	Months Duration	Consensus Cause	Party in office
1937	13	General economic	Dem
1945	8	Decline in government spending after WWII	Dem
1948	11	General economic	Dem
1953	10	Post-Korean contraction; fed policy changes	Rep
1958	8	Fed policy changes	Rep
1960	10	General economic	Dem
1969	11	Fed policy changes	Dem
1973	16	Radical shift in oil prices by OPEC	Rep
Early 1980s	12	Iranian revolution drove oil prices up; fed policy changes	Dem
Early 1990s	8	Fed policy changes; oil prices	Rep
Early 2000s	8	Bust of dot-com bubble; 9/11 terrorist attacks	Rep
Late 2000s	Ongoing	Collapse of housing and banking; dramatic increases in oil prices	Rep

During this seventy-plus-year period, six Democratic presidents have been in the White House, for a total of forty-one years, and six Republicans have held the presidency, for a total of thirty-five years. It is worth noting that since 1973, four of the recessions have been attributed to shocks or dramatic shifts in oil prices and supply. It's little wonder that alternative energy would be a high priority for the current administration. In reality, it should have been a high priority of every administration since 1973. Where has our elected political leadership's focus on energy independence been since 1973? In 1977, the Carter administration established the Department of Energy (DOE). It consolidated a number of existing entities into a single department. One of the DOE's initial tasks, and one that is still at the top of their mission statement, was to reduce our nation's dependence on oil. This year their budget is $26.4 billion and we are not much closer today than we were in 1977 to finding alternative energy sources, but we sure like to talk about it. How many more oil crises will our nation encounter before a real effort is made to reduce our dependence on foreign oil?

At the time that President Obama's 2010 budget was delivered to Congress, the current recession had persisted for over thirteen months. In excess of 3.6 million jobs, including over 200,000 auto industry jobs, had been lost. His budget address pointed out that manufacturing jobs are at their lowest level since 1946 (manufacturing employment peaked in the early '80s and has been declining since). While both points the president makes are true, the report fails to identify what actions will be taken by the government to change the current employment trend. Labor costs, pension costs, medical costs, and environmental-regulatory costs have contributed to making products manufactured in the United States uncompetitive when compared to foreign alternatives. There is no mention that many of the nations that are manufacturing goods for export to the United States are not subject to abide by similar laws and rules that our government has forced on domestic manufacturers. Based on the laws that are currently being proposed, it appears that our politicians are oblivious to the fact that there is a cost associated with every regulation. These costs are ultimately priced into the finished product and paid for by the consumer, the American taxpayer. The end result of these regulatory actions is that many American products can no longer compete in the global marketplace. Couple these factors with the reduced labor costs that most underdeveloped and developing nations enjoy and it's understandable why the United States has witnessed the continued decline in its manufacturing base. There is absolutely nothing being done that is going to change this trend anytime soon, and passage of additional restrictive legislation will only accelerate the decline.

A direct result of the continued attrition of the manufacturing base is the erosion of our middle class. From our nation's earliest days, it has been the middle class that has sustained our country and our economy. The jobs of this class have not gone away or been eliminated; they have simply gone elsewhere. During the last eight years, China saw its manufacturing base increase by ten million workers while the United

States saw its manufacturing base decrease by over three million workers.

Instead of looking to place blame, our leaders should be looking at how our current tax codes and federal and state regulations are impacting the price of American-made products and should be identifying what steps could be taken to level the global playing field. The impact of future recessions could be lessened if American workers are fully employed and producing products that are priced to compete globally. Laws and regulations that our politicians impose on American industries are necessary, but they should be examining how to mitigate the "Legislative and Tax" penalties on American-made products to allow them to be more competitive. Regardless of what the pundits advocate, the last twenty years have demonstrated the risks associated with not having a strong, vibrant manufacturing base. In 1992, during Ross Perot's run for the presidency, many found his prediction of "a nation of burger flippers" humorous. Today it is anything but. The United States must have the ability to provide jobs for people willing to put in a hard day's work. Securing a college education is no longer a guarantee of employment, and even those with degrees are finding that the wages in the service industries are not on parity with the income generated by a strong manufacturing sector. The government needs to focus on maintaining and restoring manufacturing jobs, not creating additional obstacles that manufacturers, and in particular small businesses, must overcome. As a consuming nation and a net importer, we are running the risk of being held hostage by foreign manufacturers much like our oil dependence experiences since 1973.

In addition to the social-economic benefits, a strong manufacturing base is critical to our national security. Remember in the early days of the global war on terrorism when we could not get ceramic vest plates for our troops? The reason was that we did not have a manufacturing base that was capable of meeting the demand. We ended up solving the problem by purchasing the product from a European ally.

To mention the 2008–2009 recession without mentioning the 2008 oil crisis that our nation, as well as the world, encountered would be an injustice. For 2005, 2006, and the first half of 2007, oil prices were in the $60 to the mid-$70 range per barrel. Between September 2007 and July of 2008, prices escalated from about $75 per barrel to over $145 per barrel, an increase of 93 percent. During this time, we saw gas prices increase to over $4.00 per gallon. This increase had a disproportional impact on low-income and middle-income earners, making it more difficult for them to meet their fixed financial obligations, such as house and car payments.

The impact that the oil price increases had on the economy is more significant than many of the people we have surveyed understand. According to the *CIA World Fact Book*, global daily oil consumption is approximately eighty-five million barrels. The United States is the number one oil consumer in the world, using nearly 20.7 million barrels daily. However, the United States produces only 8.5 million barrels per day, which means that we need to purchase an additional 12.2 million barrels of foreign oil each and every day.

Cost of Oil Assumptions:
20.7 million barrels of oil are consumed daily in the United States.
110 million families reside in the United States.

	Oil Price	Total Cost of Oil per Day	Annual Increase per Family
9/1/2007	$75	$1,552,500,000	
9/1/2008	$145	$3,001,500,000	$4,808
Average Price	$107	$2,214,900,000	$2,198

From September 2007 to September 2008, oil prices averaged $107 per barrel. This increase over the $75 price amounted to a nearly a $242 billion increase in annual oil expenditures, or approximately an increase of $2,198 per family per year. At its peak of $145 per barrel during the summer of 2008, oil price increases consumed $4,808 of disposable income per family on an annualized basis. Even though the oil price increases did not remain at those levels, the price spikes resulted in a greater portion of disposal income being reallocated to meet the rising oil costs. That reallocation had a ripple effect throughout the economy. The magnitude and speed of the change caused unrest and concerns, resulting in a retreat in spending. With less money to spend, there were fewer items bought. This reduced the need for manufactured products, which ultimately reduced the workforce. All along the way, peripheral businesses and people were impacted. Eventually this downward spiral led to an economic slowdown and ultimately contributed to the current recession.

There is no easy answer to our nation's energy dependence and certainly no solution on the visible horizon. During the current oil crisis, many in Congress were advocating the use of the U.S. strategic oil reserve as a way to control prices. This is an example of shifting the metrics (gauging tools) in an effort to distort reality and does little if anything to provide a meaningful solution to the problem. Here is the impact of using the U.S. strategic oil reserve: Our strategic oil reserve consists of approximately 725 million barrels of oil, which sounds like a big number. But the simple math tells us that this reserve would cover our oil import requirements for fifty-nine days (725 barrels/12.2 barrels of imported oil consumed per day). Given these numbers, it is clear that the strategic oil reserve is not really strategic and cannot replace our need for imported oil or mitigate spikes in pricing. Without question, suggesting the strategic oil reserve as a solution is a mathematically absurd proposition.

Oil has contributed to four of the recessions since 1973, yet in 2009 our nation is still as dependent on foreign oil as it was in 1973. Who has failed? If the government is going to place restrictions on drilling and refining capacity, should they not promote the development of cost-effective alternative-energy policies to protect its citizens and national interest? Delving into the issues surrounding energy, although important, would digress from the focus of this book. Suffice it to say that with all of the technology that has been developed and money invested over the last forty years, this problem should have been addressed in a meaningful way.

Considering past recessions, it is highly likely that the next recession will be directly attributable to governmental actions or to a lack thereof.

AFFORDABLE HOUSING AND THE HOUSING CRISIS

A FAILED GOVERNMENT MANDATE

In his 2010 budget, President Obama discussed the impact the current recession has had on the American worker. He went on to discuss how the meltdown in the capital and the credit markets is a major reason for the recession. There is absolutely no question that those in the working class or those on fixed income were disproportionally impacted by the housing, capital, and credit market meltdowns that contributed to the recession that started in 2008. What has not been widely discussed is a major cause of the 2008–2009 subprime credit-market meltdown. It was largely driven by congressional mandates to expand home ownership to the very group of people it ended up hurting. Congressional mandates prompted the proliferation of innovative financing tools and relaxed lending requirements to support home ownership mandates. Many citizens, politicians, and the media advocated that capital market greed played a significant role in the housing crisis. Unquestionably, greed contributed to some degree in the financial crisis we encountered. Greed has been a problem throughout history, but attempting to lay the problem at the door of the banking industry is disingenuous, superficial, and simply misleading.

The president attributed the credit crisis to "irresponsible lending to thousands of Americans, who when offered the chance to own their own home, were advised to throw caution to the wind." Caution was indeed thrown to the wind, and the driving force can be traced to the actions of Congress.

Home ownership has long been a governmental priority with the first government sponsored enterprise (GSE), the Farm Credit System, being created by Congress in 1916. Today, GSEs are a group of financial services corporations whose function is to increase capital availability (money available to borrowers) and reduce the cost of credit to low-income families, minority groups, and targeted geographic areas. GSE's first venture into the home mortgage segment came with the creation of the Federal Home Loan Banks in 1932.

Today there are four housing sector GSEs: Federal Home Loan Banks, Federal National Mortgage Association (1938) (Fannie Mae), Government National Mortgage Association (1968) (Ginnie Mae), and Federal Home Loan Mortgage Corporation (1970) (Freddie Mac). These financial institutions were created primarily to act as a financial conduit to assist lenders and borrowers in acquiring housing and agricultural land. These GSEs have created a secondary market for mortgage loans through guarantees, bonding, and securitization. This secondary market allowed banks, mortgage companies, and other primary market lenders to increase their loan volume, which perpetuated the rise in mortgage-backed securities that were bundled and sold to investors. In other words, while the concept of mortgage-backed securities provides an aura of security, we now know, and should have known, that they are not without risk. When a borrower has little, if any, equity in a home, and loans are made assuming that housing prices will continue to escalate, we have a recipe for disaster.

In the early '90s, Congress created an initiative to narrow the gap in those able to afford home ownership by making the American dream of home ownership more accessible to lower-income families, in particular minorities and immigrants. At its inception, the risk associated with the program was clearly identified and known. In a 1999 *New York Times* article on the subject, Washington bureau editor Steven A. Holmes noted that "in moving, even tentatively, into this new area of lending, Fannie Mae is taking on significantly more risk, which may not pose any difficulties during flush economic times. But the government-subsidized corporation may run into trouble in an economic downturn, prompting a government rescue similar to that of the savings and loan industry in the 1980s." Obviously many overlooked the sage advice contained in this article.

HUD (Housing and Urban Development) established housing goals in accordance with the Federal Housing Enterprises Financial Safety and Soundness Act of 1992 (the 1992 GSE Act). The act charged the GSEs to make loans more accessible by instructing HUD to establish three goals:

1. A broad low-income and moderate-income goal for families with less than the area median income
2. A geographically targeted goal for housing located in underserved areas, such as low-income and high-minority census tracks
3. A targeted income-based goal for special affordable housing; housing that is affordable to very low-income families and low-income families living in low-income areas

In 1996, the GSEs developed specific performance goals for each of these targets. In late 1999, to facilitate meeting the escalating goals, Fannie Mae and Freddie Mac, both GSEs and the nation's largest home mortgage underwriters, relaxed their lending standards to include those with credit scores that were just a "notch below" traditional underwriting standards (subprime borrowers) and at the same time reduced down-payment requirements. Over time the "notch below" was expanded to several notches. To remain competitive, non-GSE lenders were forced to modify their lending requirements, which opened the entire mortgage system to additional risk. These changes in lending standards increased housing demand and resulted in the explosion of the subprime industry. It is estimated that the program resulted in 7.5 million subprime mortgages being issued with a total value of $1.3 trillion. Currently, the U.S. Census Bureau estimates that one out of five home mortgages originated since 1999 have zero or negative equity.

Skyrocketing loan volume was supported by secondary markets in the form of bundled mortgage securities. The sale of these securities increased the liquidity (cash available for additional loans) to the mortgage industry. The secondary markets allowed the mortgages to be sold, which in turn provided additional liquidity, which allowed more loans to be originated. The cycle was self-perpetuating. Investors purchasing these bundled securities were investing in obligations, believing that they were secure. This belief was flawed, because in many cases there was no equity or minimal equity in the properties. This was because down payment requirements were either eliminated or substantially scaled back. The fact that many of the securities were insured by the likes of AIG and others created the false assumption that the securities had little risk. This perceived lower risk served to allay the concerns of the investment community as well and allowed the securities to be marketed. The market thrived and provided additional cash that flowed back into the mortgage market. The insurance models were built on historical risk, which did not include the risks associated with the expansion and inclusion of the relaxed standards of subprime borrowers. The entire program was doomed to fail. It was just a matter of when.

Not surprisingly, the GSE lending goals were exceeded by both Fannie Mae and Freddie Mac every year. The following chart depicts how each of the goals changed between 1996 and 2005. It is interesting to note that the emphasis shifted to a higher percentage of loans being channeled into low- and moderate-income applicants, which would exacerbate the downside financial risk in the event of an economic downturn.

	1996 Goal	2005 Goal
Low- and moderate-income goal	40%	50%
Geographic-underserved area	22%	30%
Special-affordable goal, low-income families in low-income areas	38%	20%

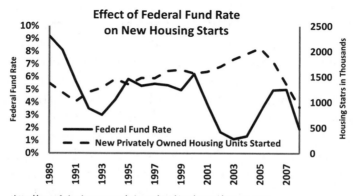

http://www.federalreserve.gov/releases/H15/data/Annual/H15_FF_O.txt
http://www.census.gov/const/startsan.pdf

It is clear that the GSE social engineering project of Bill Clinton and Congress contributed significantly to the problem by attempting to artificially expand home ownership. If anything, this entire process demonstrates the dynamic nature of the capital market. The markets found a way to package the loan products and raise capital, which is exactly what capital markets are supposed to do. The capital market was not responsible for forecasting interest rate levels or the timing of interest rate changes, the date of the next recession, or even future employment levels. Lenders did not make anyone buy a home who did not want to buy one. They simply facilitated the social mandates of Congress.

Although lenders and insurers are not without fault, congressional mandates contributed significantly to the housing crisis.

CASH FOR CLUNKERS
WAS THE MONEY WELL SPENT?

The Car Allowance Rebate Systems (CARS), or what was commonly known as the "Cash for Clunkers" program, was an attempt by the government to stimulate the automotive market. According to Speaker Pelosi (go to YouTube and do a search on Pelosi "Cash for Clunkers"), the goal of the program was to increase automotive sales and help the environment by having newer cars on the road. The government allocated $3 billion in taxpayer money to a program designed to accelerate automotive sales by providing new car buyer trade-in incentives ranging from $3,500 to $4,500 toward the purchase of a new passenger vehicle. The government and the automotive industry hailed the program as a great success. But was it really?

An analysis of the program by Edmunds.com, which distributes automotive information via the Web, reveals that the program had far less impact on auto sales than was reported by the government. According to Edmunds.com, the true cost of the program was closer to $24,000 per car. Why the gap? It is all about the measurement tools and how they are used. The government claim of success is based on the number of voucher applications it processed. According to government numbers, approximately 685,000 program vouchers were processed. The government reported that the program generated incremental sales of 685,000 vehicles. An incremental sale is defined as a sale that is in addition to what would have been expected, based on the economic conditions.

Edmunds.com looked at historical sales data, current market conditions, sales in subsequent periods, and several other factors in an attempt to identify the incremental number of vehicles sold as a result of the program. According to Edmunds.com, the calculated number of incremental vehicle sales was 125,000 and not the 685,000 reported by the government. Using the Edmunds.com analysis, which takes into account more logical data than just the total vouchers processed, the cost of the program was approximately $24,000 ($3 billion /125,000) per vehicle versus the $3,500 to $4,500 target.

The other part of this program was purported to be environmentally motivated. Let's examine the potential environmental benefits the program generated. According to the Department of Transportation, in 2008 there were 244 million highway-registered vehicles. of which 135 million were classified as passenger cars. Replacing 685,000 environmentally unfriendly vehicles resulted in replacing approximately 0.28 percent (that's slightly more than one-quarter of 1 percent) of the total vehicle population. Does anybody, other than the politicians who passed the bill, really believe that replacing one-quarter of 1 percent of the total vehicle population is going to have a significant impact on the environment? Couple the small percentage of vehicles replaced with the fact that $2 billion of the funding for the "Cash for Clunkers" program came from a program that was intended to back loans for renewable energy company research, and the "environmental" impact touted by the government seems more like political rhetoric than substantive results.

While the intent of the program was to promote new car sales, it had a couple of unintended consequences. The traffic in auto dealers slowed dramatically after the program expired, supporting the analysis that many of the sales were not incremental. The program also suffered from the law of unintended consequences as it depleted the available used car inventory, thus driving the price for used cars higher. These higher prices impacted those who purchase used cars the most, the low- and middle-income families. Many felt compelled by the prospects of free cash to replace their clunkers when it is typically less expensive in the long run to repair a vehicle you already own. The purchase either used available cash or credit, both of which took money out of the hands of the buying public in an economy where many were already financially strapped.

But the "fuzzy math" does not stop there. Our nation is currently running a deficit and is expected to do so until at least 2020, per President Obama's own ten-year budget. The cost of "Cash for Clunkers" is going to be financed, and the interest will continually be paid for at least ten years. Assuming that the interest rate of Treasury securities averages 5 percent over the next ten years, the incremental interest cost for "Cash for Clunkers" is going to be an additional $1.88 billion. That's right—what started as a $3 billion dollar program will realistically cost taxpayers closer to $5 billion by the time payments are finally completed.

Was "Cash for Clunkers" money well spent or was it just another government clunker?

THE EVOLUTION OF TAXES

DO HIGHER TAXES LEAD TO GOVERNMENT EXPANSION, OR DOES GOVERNMENT EXPANSION LEAD TO HIGHER TAXES?

The way politicians change taxes and the impact those changes have on our nation's taxpayers is similar to boiling frogs. You put frogs into cool water and turn on the heat, and before the frogs realize what is happening, they're cooked. Without realizing the impact, taxpayers are getting cooked as well. Parkinson's Law states, "Work expands so as to fill the time available for its completion." Adapting Parkinson's Law to government budgets would result in spending expanding to equal the revenues it collects. As a government collects more, it would spend more. Our government, however, has invalidated Parkinson's Law by spending in excess of the tax revenues for the past forty years and continues to show no signs of controlling its spending.

The point is not to bore you with a lot of tax history; there is no need for that. While much has been written about the impact that taxes have on economic growth or contraction, the evidence seems to support the proposition that lower taxes result in an acceleration of economic growth.

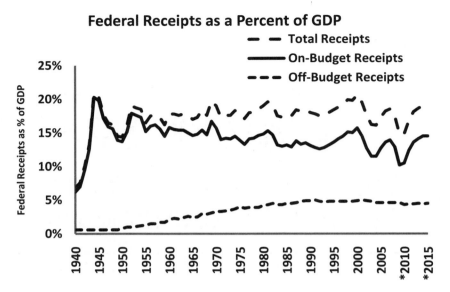

Federal Receipts as a Percent of GDP

– – Total Receipts
—— On-Budget Receipts
- - - Off-Budget Receipts

* Estimate   Table 1.2—SUMMARY OF RECEIPTS, OUTLAYS, AND
SURPLUSES OR DEFICITS (–) AS PERCENTAGES OF GDP: 1940–2015
http://www.whitehouse.gov/omb/budget/Historicals/

At the turn of the nineteenth century, federal tax revenues were 1.5 percent of Gross Domestic Product (GDP). Over the last forty years, tax revenues have averaged 18.3 percent of GDP. In 2008, federal tax revenues stood at nearly 18 percent of GDP. This means that about $0.18 of every $1 generated in the U.S. economy goes to the federal government in the form of taxes. It is highly probable that that number will grow, as the government will turn to tax increases to avoid going even deeper into debt.

Between 1870 and 1913, almost 90 percent of all revenues collected at the federal level were the result of excise tax collections, primarily from tobacco and alcohol. The top rate in 1916 was 15 percent on those earning in excess of $1.5 million; in 1917 the rate increased to 16 percent on those over $40,000, and the top rate was 67 percent on those earning over $1.5 million. Just to provide a reference point, $40,000 of income in 1917 would equate to over $3.2 million of income today using a 5 percent growth rate.

Top marginal rates increased and varied from 70 percent to over 90 percent from the '40s to the mid '60s. From the mid '60s to the early '80s, top marginal rates declined to the 50 percent level. In the late

'80s, top marginal rates decreased to slightly under 40 percent. Currently we have a top rate of 35 percent on those with taxable income over $357,000. It is clear that the government is collecting a larger percentage of individual earnings than they did at the turn of the century by a significant margin.

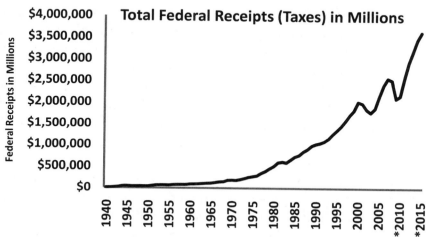

* Estimate   Table 1.1—Summary of Receipts, Outlays, and Surpluses or Deficits (-) 1789-2015
http://www.whitehouse.gov/omb/budget/Historicals/

Increasing revenue, which in reality is increasing taxes, has historically been the answer to all government maladies. The largest single source of tax revenue is derived from individual income taxes. The government's appetite for taxation is not limited to just the federal government, as state and local governments are evaluating taxation alternatives to solve their budget woes. We are not going to make an excursion into the budget problems of state and local governments, but you should recognize that most state budgets are another potential burden for both taxpayers and the economy. It is currently estimated that forty-seven states are experiencing varying degrees of financial difficulty.

The government collects revenue in the form of taxes and redistributes that revenue on programs it deems appropriate. Taxpayers need to be concerned with both the expanse and appropriateness of what is being collected and redistributed. Those on the receiving end believe they are entitled to more. Those on the paying end feel they are being unjustly taxed. There is no chance of agreement while the two sides are so diametrically opposed. The balance shifts when one side or the other has more voting power. When more people find themselves in financial difficulty, they look to the government for solutions. This shifts the balance of power away from the taxpayer.

Currently, Greece is experiencing the effects of out-of-control spending and rising deficits. Greek citizens are asking their government to continue benefits and entitlement payments that the government cannot afford to provide. The European Union (EU) has mandated that the government of Greece reduce entitlement programs and increase taxes to maintain their membership in the EU. This severely limited the government's ability to satisfy the demands of its citizens, which now has prompted social unrest throughout the country.

It is important to remember that the primary source of revenue the government has is taxes. Printing money is not a source of revenue and ultimately becomes a source of both inflation and devaluation. The act of simply printing additional money cannot go on indefinitely, as the currency ultimately becomes worthless as the risk of hyperinflation grows. Those unfamiliar with the term hyperinflation should do a Web search on the history of the currencies of Mexico and South American countries during the '70s and '80s.

The government's thirst for taxes has grown and must continue to grow if it continues to assume more and more responsibility over the lives of its citizens.

SOURCES OF REVENUE
IS THERE REALLY A MONEY TREE?

In the 2008 GFY (government fiscal year), the federal government had tax revenues of $2.524 trillion. The sources of revenues, in billions of dollars, for 2008 were:

Individual Income Taxes	$1,146	45%
Corporate Income Taxes	$304	12%
Social Insurance Taxes	$900	36%
Excise Tax	$67	3%
Estate and Gift Tax	$29	1%
Customs and Duties	$28	1%
Miscellaneous Receipts	$50	2%
Total	$2,524	100%

*This is in billions; a thousand billion equals a trillion.

The sources of tax revenues have been somewhat constant since 1970, with the exception of Social Insurance. Social Insurance, a combination of Social Security and Medicare, has increased by nearly 57 percent since 1970, due to a combination of increases in rates and the earnings base that is subject to the tax (more on that later).

Sources of Tax Revenue for:				
	1970	1980	1990	2008
Individual	47%	47%	45%	45%
Corporate	17%	12%	9%	12%
Social Insurance	23%	31%	37%	36%
All other	13%	10%	9%	7%

The information contained in these two tables reveals some very interesting points.

1. The single largest source of taxation is at the individual level.
2. In 2008, individuals paid 63 percent of all taxes when income and employee Social Insurance taxes are combined. Social Insurance taxes are split between employees and employers, meaning that each is paying 18 percent of the total.
3. If the employer portion of the Social Insurance tax is included, the individual tax number goes to 81 percent.

A logical question is "Should corporate entities be paying a higher amount of taxes?" The simple answer is no. While a corporate tax increase is always a popular political suggestion and would indeed increase tax revenue, it would ultimately create a far greater financial burden on lower-income groups. Increasing corporate income taxes is a form of regressive taxation. Corporations would simply build the higher cost of the tax into the price of their goods and services, therefore passing that incremental cost on to the consumer. Another option would be for them to absorb the incremental cost, which would result in lower earnings or reduce their ability to pay dividends to shareholders. The consequence of both would be lower stock prices.

When you hear references to increasing taxes on corporations, know that those costs will most likely be passed on to the consumer in the form of price increases. They will disproportionally impact individuals with lower incomes, who can least afford to pay the tax. This is why our current tax system captures income taxes at the individual level, where the ability to pay can be factored into the tax rate structure.

The following chart illustrates the regressive impact of a gasoline tax increase. This is applicable to either a direct increase in gas taxes or indirect business tax increases, which are ultimately passed on to the consumer.

Adjusted Gross Income (AGI)	$100,000	$50,000
Amount spent on gas annually	$1,500	$1,500
Percent of AGI	1.5%	3.0%
Government increases gas taxes by 15%		
Amount spent annually after tax increase	$1,725	$1,725
Percent of AGI	1.7%	3.5%
Percent Increase	13.3%	16.6%

While both individuals have the same $225 increase in annual gas costs, the tax hike results in an increase of 16.6 percent on the lower-income individual versus 13.3 percent for the higher-income individual. The same logic will apply to any corporate tax increase that becomes baked into the price of the product. There is no question that the government will want to increase taxes to avoid growing the national debt, but the masses should not want those taxes to be in the form of corporate taxes.

No, there is not a money tree. The individual American taxpayer, either directly or indirectly, will pay 100 percent of the tax burden.

WHO PAYS AND HOW MUCH

IF 47 MILLION FILERS DIDN'T PAY ANY TAXES IN 2007, THEN WHO DID?

We have examined the government's sources of revenue (taxes). Now we are going to identify those sources by income and show who really did pay the taxes.

According to 2007 IRS information, which is the most recent year that complete data is available, there were 142.9 million tax returns filed, with a combined total net adjusted gross income (AGI) of $8.7 trillion. Individual taxpayers paid a total of $1.1 trillion in taxes in 2007. This equates to an average collection rate of 12.8% of AGI (total income tax collected/total AGI). Taxable income would be a more appropriate denominator, but we will use AGI, as that is what is used in the IRS data.

While there were 142.9 million returns filed in 2007, taxes were collected on only 96.2 million returns, meaning that 46.7 million returns paid no income taxes. This equates to almost a third of all returns filed having no tax liability. This statistic does not include those individuals who did not file a tax return in 2007. Including that group would obviously increase the percentage of taxpayers who paid no taxes in 2007.

The following table shows the number of returns, the net AGI level, and the taxes paid by various income levels for 2005–2007. This table includes only those returns that had a tax liability, meaning they paid some amount of taxes.

———————————— Net Adjusted Gross Income ————————————

2007	under $50,000	$50,000 under $100,000	$100,000 under $200,000
Taxable Returns in (000s)	47,082	31,195	13,458
% of total	48.90%	32.40%	14.00%
Net AGI in millions	$1,837,047	$2,210,446	$1,793,040
% of total	21.10%	25.40%	20.60%
Taxes Paid in millions	$86,622	$190,715	$228,688
% of total	7.80%	17.10%	20.50%
Tax % of AGI	4.70%	8.60%	12.80%

———————————— Net Adjusted Gross Income ————————————

2006	under $50,000	$50,000 under $100,000	$100,000 under $200,000
Taxable Returns in (000s)	47,845	28,799	12,041
% of total	51.60%	31.10%	13.00%
Net AGI in millions	$1,293,011	$2,044,851	$1,600,506
% of total	17.40%	27.50%	21.50%
Taxes Paid in millions	$85,757	$184,463	$209,381
% of total	8.40%	18.00%	20.40%
Tax % of AGI	6.60%	9.00%	13.10%

———————————— Net Adjusted Gross Income ————————————

2005	under $50,000	$50,000 under $100,000	$100,000 under $200,000
Taxable Returns in (000s)	48,447	27,821	10,767
% of total	53.50%	30.70%	11.90%
Net AGI in millions	$1,298,986	$1,967,468	$1,425,108
% of total	18.90%	28.70%	20.80%
Taxes Paid in millions	$86,798	$178,811	$189,468
% of total	9.30%	19.10%	20.30%
Tax % of AGI	6.70%	9.10%	13.30%

2007	Net Adjusted Gross Income		
	$200,000 under $500,000	$500,000 under $100,0000	$1,000,000 or more
Taxable Returns in (000s)	3,492	651	392
% of total	3.60%	0.70%	0.40%
Net AGI in millions	$1,004,659	$441,439	$1,401,088
% of total	11.60%	5.10%	16.10%
Taxes Paid in millions	$196,381	$103,163	$310,033
% of total	17.60%	9.20%	27.80%
Tax % of AGI	19.50%	23.40%	22.10%

2006	Net Adjusted Gross Income		
	$200,000 under $500,000	$500,000 under $100,0000	$1,000,000 or more
Taxable Returns in (000s)	3,115	588	353
% of total	3.40%	0.60%	0.40%
Net AGI in millions	$893,337	$398,745	$1,209,023
% of total	12.00%	5.40%	16.30%
Taxes Paid in millions	$177,041	$94,214	$273,064
% of total	17.30%	9.20%	26.70%
Tax % of AGI	19.80%	23.60%	22.60%

2005	Net Adjusted Gross Income		
	$200,000 under $500,000	$500,000 under $100,0000	$1,000,000 or more
Taxable Returns in (000s)	2,732	523	303
% of total	3.00%	0.60%	0.30%
Net AGI in millions	$787,269	$354,471	$1,023,421
% of total	11.50%	5.20%	14.90%
Taxes Paid in millions	$159,395	$84,700	$235,664
% of total	17.10%	9.10%	25.20%
Tax % of AGI	20.20%	23.90%	23.00%

Using this information, we developed the following table to aggregate or combine statistics for the filing group with AGI in excess of $200,000. This table shows:

> The percent of filers
> The percent of the group's AGI as a percent of the total AGI for all taxpayers
> The percent of the total taxes paid for the group and the tax rate for the group

The group of wage earners earning in excess of $200,000 has grown by less than 1 percent over the last three years. Contrary to what is often quoted, there is no explosion in the "wealthy" population, defined as those making over $200,000 per year. Likewise there is no explosion in income, as their percent of the total income has increased by 1.2 percent over the same period. This indicates that the group's income level is not skyrocketing, as some suggest. In fact, using simple ratios, you would mathematically expect their percent of the total AGI to be closer to 38 percent of the total versus the actual percent of 32.8 percent. This indicates a reduction in the dollar level of income for the group. The following table indicates that this group paid 3.3 percent more of the 2007 total burden than they paid in 2005. In 2007, 4.7 percent of taxpayers paid nearly 55 percent of all taxes. Expanding this group to 10 percent reveals that this group of taxpayers paid over 70 percent of all taxes.

Filers with AGI in excess of $200,000

	2007	2006	2005
% of all filers with tax liability	4.7%	4.4%	3.9%
% of all filers income	32.8%	33.6%	31.6%
% of total taxes paid	54.6%	53.2%	51.3%
Tax rate % of AGI	21.6%	21.7%	22.1%

The argument that this income group is paying less tax is simply not supported by the facts.

Let's look at the total taxes paid and the tax rate as a percent of AGI for those making under $50,000.

Filers with AGI less than $50,000

	2007	2006	2005
% of all filers with tax liability	48.90%	51.60%	53.50%
% of all filers income	21.10%	17.40%	18.90%
% of total taxes paid	7.80%	8.40%	9.30%
Tax rate % of AGI	4.70%	6.60%	6.70%

It is clear that the $50,000 and under group is continuing to decline as a percent of all filers, which is a positive trend as they are moving to higher-income groups. The percent of all filers' income for this group is increasing, while the percent of the total taxes paid and the tax rate percent of AGI has declined. The data simply does not support that this group's tax burden has increased and in fact shows the opposite. In 2007, this group paid 1.5 percent less of the total tax burden than they did in 2005.

Analyzing this information from the IRS Web site supports that there is no evidence that taxpayers with an AGI in excess of $200,000 are paying less at the expense of those at lower income levels. The $200,000 and over group is paying nearly 55 percent of all taxes. Are there individuals who make hundreds of thousands and millions of dollars in income and pay no taxes? The answer is yes, but that is the exception. If Congress wants to choose to close the tax loopholes that allow these exceptions to continue, it has the power to do so. Congress will most likely not close these loopholes, as this group includes some of the largest political campaign contributors.

There is one glaring question that pops out of the data. Based on their income, an argument could be made that the group earning over $1 million has the greatest ability to pay, yet their 2007 average rate of 22.1 percent is less than the group making $500k to $1 million, which had an average rate of 23.4 percent. Clearly taxes are not equal at the high-income level either. That is not a taxpayer problem but a congressional problem, as they approve the tax code.

The data shows that despite the rhetoric, a few are paying a whole lot.

TAXES AND THE DEFICIT
WILL INCREASING TAXES ELIMINATE THE DEFICIT?

As economist Milton Friedman said, "Congress can raise taxes because it can persuade a sizable fraction of the populace that somebody else will pay."

Given that President Obama is expecting our nation to incur deficits until at least 2020, we need to look at the spending and tax changes that would be required to eradicate the annual deficits that continue to add to our national debt. With all of the moving parts, it is virtually impossible to estimate the annual deficit. The complexity is evidenced by the February 2001 projections made by the Congressional Budget Office (CBO). The CBO is the nonpartisan agency charged with reviewing budgets and legislative initiatives with budgetary implications for Congress. In 2001, the CBO projected that annual budget surpluses would increase over the next ten years to $5.6 trillion. The deficit from 2002 to 2011 is now projected at $6 trillion, which is a variance of nearly $12 trillion. Did the CBO mislead Congress? No, the CBO knows that politicians make changes, so they incorporate the disclaimer "absent new legislation and under current policies" as a way to alert readers that the numbers are based on current assumptions. When policies and circumstances are changed, it renders the previous set of the projections useless. This $12 trillion swing is an example of how massive the changes can be. Somebody has to pay for this mess. Given that no one has a clue of how much spending can or will be cut or how much taxes need to be increased, we will make assumptions about future spending and tax levels to illustrate the magnitude of the problem.

Over the last eight years, and after normalizing outlays for expenditures relating to the global war on terrorism (GWOT), the data would suggest that a realistic estimate of the average deficit would be in the $350 to $400 billion range. Analyzing the national debt from 1970 to 2007 reveals that the debt increased by an average of $226 billion per year during this thirty-seven-year period. Given the increase in entitlements as well as the increased aging population, it would seem that $350 to $400 billion would be a reasonable estimate. However, current budget projections are more than double the estimate we are using in our example.

The 2010 budget, presented by President Obama in February 2009, projected average on-budget deficits of approximately $886 billion through 2019. For illustration purposes, assume that tax increases have to cover $400 billion of the deficit, while the balance of the deficit is eliminated with spending cuts. Hopefully, a $400 billion tax increase will not be necessary for numerous reasons, but using that number demonstrates the magnitude of the problem.

According to the IRS, $1.115 trillion in individual income taxes were collected in 2007. Generating an additional $400 billion in taxes would require a 36 percent increase in individual tax rates. Current discussions have centered around increases on those making in excess of $200,000, meaning that tax rates would then increase substantially for 4.7 percent of all taxpayers. Individual income tax is not the only source of individual taxes. Remember that a full 36 percent of social taxes that are collected are also paid by individuals and their employers. Only 19 percent of all taxes collected come from nonindividual sources. That 19 percent is most likely passed on to consumers via higher prices. As discussed earlier, the other options of reducing dividends or earnings are not as likely as they would reduce stock prices.

The following statistics represent all taxpayers and the subset of those making over $200,000 annually. Individual taxpayers encompass all individual filing categories. Again, it is important to note that these numbers represent only those who file taxes. There are many in our country who have never filed a tax return and pay no taxes. If the objective is to generate an additional $400 billion in revenue, what is the impact on the wealthy, defined by many in Congress as those making over $200,000 annually?

Tax statistics for all individual taxpayers for the 2007 tax year

Number of returns—in millions	96.3
AGI for all taxpayers—$ trillions	$8.7
Taxes paid by all taxpayers—$ trillion	$1.1
Tax rate (taxes paid /AGI)	12.8%

Statistics for those earning in excess of $200K for the 2007 tax year

Number of returns—in millions	4.5
AGI—$ trillion	$2.8
Taxes paid—$ billion	$610
Percent of all returns	4.7%
Percent of total AGI	32%
Percent of all taxes paid	55%
Tax rate (taxes paid/AGI)	22%

If the government wants to increase the tax burden on the over $200,000 group by $400 billion the new statistics would be:

Statistics on those earning in excess of $200K for 2007 tax year, including a $400 billion tax increase

AGI—$ trillion	$2.8
Taxes paid—$ billion	$1,010
Percent of returns	4.7%
Percent of AGI	32%
Percent of taxes paid	67%
Tax rate (taxes paid/AGI)	36.7%

Increasing taxes to the group earning over $200,000 to generate an additional $400 billion in taxes revenues would result in that group paying 67 percent of all income taxes collected. It would also result in their tax rate increasing by 61 percent, to 36 percent from 22 percent. This would mean that 4.7 percent of the tax filers would be paying 67 percent of all individual federal income taxes, or conversely, that 95.3 percent of the filers would be paying just 33 percent of all individual taxes.

Regardless of income level, there is an appearance of inequity in this proposal. While the forty-seven million filers who pay no taxes may not have a problem with increasing taxes of the over $200,000 group by 61 percent, it's safe to say that the 4.7 percent of taxpayers being impacted would find it unacceptable. At the $200,000 income level, this would result in a $28,000 increase in taxes, which is significant by any standard.

An alternative is to increase taxes on those earning in excess of $200,000 by some percent (assume 2 percent) and implement a surtax on those earning in excess of $1 million. This group has 392,000 filers and accounted for $1.4 trillion of AGI. The following table shows the 2007 statistics for those earning in excess of $1 million.

	$1 mil under $1.5 mil	$1.5 mil under $2 mil	$2 mil under $5 mil	$5 mil under $10 mil	$10 mil or more
Taxable returns in thousands	166	71	109	28	18
% of Total	42.3%	18.1%	27.8%	7.1%	4.6%
Net AGI in millions	$200,786	$121,768	$324,593	$192,328	$561,613
% of total for grouping	14.3%	8.7%	23.2%	13.7%	40.1%
Taxes paid in millions	$48,354	$29,351	$77,555	$43,930	$110,843
% of total for grouping	15.6%	9.5%	25.0%	14.2%	35.7%
Tax % of AGI	24.1%	24.1%	23.9%	22.8%	19.7%

The distribution for 2006 was similar, with a total of 352,000 filers in the over $1 million category.

If a 5 percent surtax were levied on those with an AGI in excess of $1 million, it would generate an additional $70 billion in tax revenue. Those with an AGI in excess of $10 million make up a full 40 percent of the income of the total group, and yet they only had a tax rate of 19.7 percent. This is the lowest rate of the over $1 million group and below the 22.1 percent average for the group. If the over $10 million group were to pay an additional 5 percent surtax (10 percent total), it would generate an additional $28 billion of revenue.

The following recap shows the additional tax revenue generated from making these changes.

	Tax Generated
Increasing taxes on those making over $200,000 by 2%	$56 billion
Placing a 5% millionaire surtax on those making over $1 million	$70 billion
Placing an additional 5% tax on those making over $10 million	$28 billion
Total Taxes Generated	$154 billion

The combination of these three actions would generate $154 billion of additional income tax revenue. While this is a large number, it is still not adequate enough to generate the incremental income tax target of $400 billion that we set. If the goal is to generate $400 billion by increasing taxes, it will require a tax increase 2.5 times greater than the increases discussed earlier. At the risk of sounding negative, this exercise shows that the deficit level is getting to the point where tax increases on just the wealthy alone will not solve the problem.

These illustrations assume that only $400 billion will be needed to eliminate the average annual deficit we established. The president's ten-year budget projects an estimated average deficit of $800 billion per year. For these numbers to work, the government would also have to reduce spending by an average of $400 billion per year. We all know that spending reductions are far more difficult to make than spending increases.

Realistically, taxing the "somebody else" referenced by Milton Friedman will not solve the problem either.

OUTLAYS AND THEIR IMPACT
ON THE NATIONAL DEBT
THE GOVERNMENT LOVES TO SPEND OUR MONEY.

Medical doctors know that there is little benefit in attempting to treat the symptoms of an illness. The patient may experience temporary relief, but if the doctor fails to treat the illness, the problem will persist. It is the illness that must be identified before an appropriate course of treatments can begin. Decades of growing federal debt is the symptom of an overspending illness. The deficit of the federal government is a symptom of overspending. Federal outlays (spending) have been on a steady increase since the early '80s. During this time the nation has continued to run at a deficit.

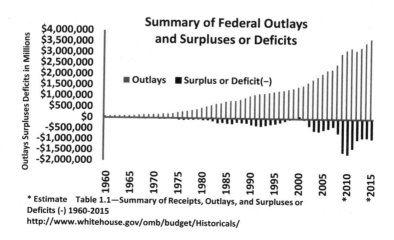

Summary of Federal Outlays and Surpluses or Deficits

* Estimate   Table 1.1—Summary of Receipts, Outlays, and Surpluses or
Deficits (-) 1960-2015
http://www.whitehouse.gov/omb/budget/Historicals/

For every dollar that annual outlays exceed annual revenue (tax receipts), there will be a dollar-for-dollar increase in the national debt. The logic applies to surpluses as well. For every dollar of revenue that is generated in excess of outlays, the government will be able to reduce the national debt by a dollar. While that has not happened in over forty years, a plan to make that happen needs to be developed soon. No magic here, as it is a dollar-for-dollar relationship in either direction.

The difference between outlays and revenues for a year will yield a deficit or surplus. The summation of all deficits and surpluses for all previous years is the national debt. The national debt is easy to determine at any point in time. It's so easy that it's unclear why there would ever be a question about the size of the national debt or the amount of a deficit in a given year. Simply go to the U.S. Treasury Web site and look at the national debt between any two periods, and the difference is either the surplus or deficit for that period. To obtain the current national debt figure follow these simple steps:

- Go to www.treasurydirect.gov
- Click "view the monthly statement of the public debt"
- Click the most current month
- Under summary, click Adobe Acrobat (.PDF)

It is just that easy and accurate.

The last year the national debt showed a decline was in 1969. It has continued to increase every year since that time. This is a fact that we will cite over and over again. For good reason, everyone needs to be aware of our national debt. This cannot be emphasized enough. As of November 2009, the United States of America had amassed a total national debt (sometimes referred to as official debt or federal debt) of nearly $12 trillion. The national debt number is expected to grow to $13.7 trillion by the end of government fiscal year 2010 (GFY). As discussed earlier, the 2010 budget projects that the national debt will be $23.1 trillion at the end of 2019. Only twelve months later, the 2011 budget forecast for year 2019 now projects the national debt at $24.5 trillion, which is an increase of $1.4 trillion.

Understand that projections, by their very nature, are based on assumptions that can potentially prove to be incorrect. Not all factors can be predicted with a high degree of certainty; therefore, there is a high probability, based on the historical inability to project accurately, that if no action is taken, the actual deficit will be significantly different than projected. History shows that in most cases the deficit will be higher than budgeted. How wrong could the projections be? Time will tell. The 2019 deficit increased by $1.4 trillion in just one budget cycle year. Keep in mind that the government currently collects approximately $2.5 trillion of revenue per year, or slightly more than $200 billion every month. A change of $1.4 trillion is a significant portion of total tax collections. This year-to-year increase clearly shows that the government has no intention of slowing spending for at least the next decade. While the budget anticipates that there will be shifts in allocations, such as from defense to Medicare, the overall spending trend continues to escalate.

Economists believe that the 2010 deficit number will probably be larger than expected due to a combination of factors.

> Lower-than-expected tax revenues because of higher-than-expected unemployment levels
> Continued unchecked spending by the government
> Increasing interest payments on growing debt

Realistically, the hole the government is digging could be much deeper than projected. A year from now, we will know the correct amount.

It does not matter what set of statistics you use to rationalize the size of the federal debt. The simple fact is that the national debt is a huge number that has continued to swell for over forty years. It cannot continue.

While many advocate the government's ability to print money as a solution to the spending problems, nothing could be further from the truth. Yes, we can and have temporarily addressed the current crisis by printing money, but continuing to print money is not a viable long-term option. No one, including sovereign nations, can continue to print currency indefinitely without risk of economic collapse due to inflation.

While borrowing has sustained our appetite for spending for the last forty years, it is not a long-term solution. Investors will eventually get tired of purchasing IOUs that are paid off with more IOUs. The

Chinese recently made several overtures to the U.S. government about its inability to control spending and the potential impact it may have on their decision to continue to purchase U.S.–issued IOUs. China is currently our nation's largest creditor. Let's be thankful for those capitalist communists!

If printing and borrowing are eliminated as solutions, the last option is the American taxpayer. In the end, taxpayers are the only source of sustainable funding that our government has. Regardless of the size of the national debt, the taxpayer is ultimately going to have to foot the bill.

The problem is obvious; yet the government tries to disguise spending and debt by creating and citing new statistics. One way the government distorts spending levels is with the use of a "unified budget." The term "unified budget" is misleading, because off-budget surpluses are used to offset on-budget deficits (on-budget and off-budget items are being unified). When off-budget (Social Security) surpluses are included with on-budget deficits, it understates the annual deficit by hundreds of billions of dollars. Given the longevity of annual deficits, it appears that it is far easier to confuse the public with multiple sets of numbers and meanings rather than addressing the root or main cause of the problem.

Gaius Petronius, first-century AD governor of Bithynia and consul (who was ordered to commit suicide) recognized a human trait that has perpetuated itself for millennia: "We trained hard, but it seemed that every time we were beginning to form into teams, we would be reorganized. I was to learn later in life that we tend to meet any new situation by reorganizing, and a wonderful method it can be for creating the illusion for progress while producing confusion, inefficiency, and demoralization." The process of reorganization as an illusion for progress is a common government tactic. They use the current analysis until it no longer supports their position. Once that happens, they simply reorganize the statistics and develop a new analysis or simply refocus entirely on another issue.

In an attempt to hide the true economic perils that our nation faces, our leaders have reorganized the statistics. They have developed new sets of measurements to support their position or have attempted to refocus attention to other issues like the environment, health care, or a host of other programs. While some issues are indeed important, they all pale in comparison to the deteriorating economic health of our country. If a politician suddenly advances a new cause or set of measurements, beware, because they likely just don't want to address the economic issues at hand.

When outlays exceed revenue, the national debt will increase regardless of how it is spun.

A NEED FOR BALANCE AND PRIORITY
HAVE WE FAILED TO INVEST, OR HAVE WE JUST SPENT UNWISELY?

As President Obama articulated in his first budget to the American people, investing in the future is critical to economic growth and the well-being of our society. Who could disagree? There is absolutely no argument that can be made to the contrary. Look at the dividends the nation enjoys today from investments made over the last seventy years. These dividends come from investments in railroads, interstate highways, dam systems, space programs, and a host of other government-supported programs. However, our leaders need to understand that there is not only a difference between spending and investing, but there is also a need for balance between the two. The premise is quite simple. If Congress wants to spend, they will have less to invest. If they want to invest, they will have less to spend. This is no different than the way taxpayers must manage their own financial resources. In actuality, the only difference is that Congress can vote to take more taxpayer dollars without the taxpayer being able to do much about it until it is again time to vote.

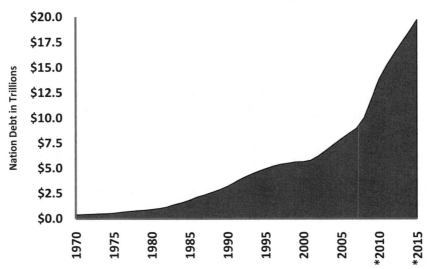

Total National Debt Outstanding in Trillions

* Estimate   Table 7.1—Federal Debt at the End of Year: 1940–2015
http://www.whitehouse.gov/omb/budget/Historicals/

If we as a nation are accused of having failed to invest, it is not because we have failed to spend, as evidenced by the preceding chart. It is a failure of our leaders, who have not spent our tax dollars wisely. Our elected representatives are in charge of spending. Many of them have been in office for several terms and have helped pass or sponsor numerous spending bills. A close examination of many representatives' voting records will often reveal a failure in fiscal responsibility, which should be an indictment against the representative's ability to manage our nation's finances and make tough economic decisions. American taxpayers are being asked by their representatives to forget the past, forgive their failings, and trust that they will be more fiscally responsible in the future. Why should American taxpayers think anything will change? Who is going to indemnify the American taxpayer for the government's failure to balance America's checkbook? At some point fiscal irresponsibility has to stop.

Over the last thirty years, federal government spending has averaged 21 percent of the nation's GDP. President Obama's 2011 budget projects that by the end of 2019, the federal government will be spending at similar or higher levels, thus driving the nation's debt toward $25 trillion. Since Congress controls spending, shouldn't this sage group be able to agree on the steps necessary to bring spending under control?

Businesses understand that all investments need to be prioritized and that all projects cannot be funded. Over the last sixty years, the government has created mandatory spending programs whose growth is legislated while at the same time continuing to add discretionary and new mandatory programs that expand spending levels without determining how they will be funded. Political leaders are just now recognizing that our economic system is not capable of funding the true cost of both the legacy programs enacted decades ago and the current and planned programs.

In the president's 2010 budget, he states that in the past, "We've been delinquent in making these down payments on future growth." How can our nation be $12 trillion in debt and be accused of failing to make a down payment?

"Down payment" is a popular term that is frequently referenced, but exactly what does it mean in a political context? We know it as an initial up-front payment that reduces the total amount borrowed on a home, car, or other purchase. What does the president want to make a down payment on? What is the ongoing payment? What are the future costs and benefits? How will we pay for future obligations? Unless these questions are fully answered, we are making a down payment on a political initiative and not a cohesive plan. In the past, Congress has made down payments on initiatives that are currently haunting today's economy. In the 1940s, our nation made a down payment on Social Security. Today that plan has an unfunded liability of at least $6.6 trillion. In the late 1960s, Congress made a down payment on Medicare. Today that plan has an unfunded liability of at least $36.4 trillion. These are only two of many legacy programs on which we have made down payments that must be funded.

Initiatives without identified sources of funding are nothing more than dreams that ultimately will become financial nightmares. Over the next ten years, the deficits will have to be funded by a combination of increased taxes, spending cuts, and incremental borrowing. As already discussed, taxing by itself is not a viable long-term option as the government cannot tax enough to control the deficit. We know that cuts in spending are difficult and seldom happen. Lenders are becoming weary of our continued borrowing.

We may have spent unwisely, but we have spent. With $13.7 trillion in debt, it is hard to argue that we failed to spend.

ON-BUDGET/OFF-BUDGET DEFICITS AND SURPLUSES

NOW YOU SEE IT; NOW YOU DON'T.

Universal Strategic Assets, Inc., a hugely profitable publicly traded company, had just reported another record quarter of profits to its shareholders. The executive team was sharing a glass of fine wine and smoking expensive cigars in the boardroom, celebrating their accomplishments. Unknown to the executive team, the company CFO had been conducting covert transactions with a related company, Acme Widgets, for several years. The CFO used these transactions to improve the financial position and financial results of Universal Strategic Assets' balance sheet and income statement. The transactions served to improve the performance of Universal Strategic Assets by creating financial transactions between Acme Widgets Company and the parent company, Universal Strategic Assets. These transactions were not recorded on the parent company's books. Had the two companies reported consolidated results, the true performance of Universal Strategic Assets would have been known to all. The transaction results were not consolidated, and by the time the deception became apparent, billions of dollars of shareholder equity had been lost.

Enron and MCI/WorldCom used similar accounting practices, and their prosecutions reaffirmed that this type of accounting is illegal. So why has Universal Strategic Assets gone unpunished? After all, they still practice this type of accounting every day. It's because

Universal Strategic Assets (USA) is not a company at all. That's right, the U.S. government moves money around, similarly to those reviled companies, between on-budget and off-budget accounts to distort the actual level of spending.

On-budget and off-budget accounting is very similar. Due to the mingling of on-budget and off-budget deficits and surpluses, discussing them together helps to clarify the relationship that exists between them and elucidates how it distorts our nation's financial picture. Essentially, on-budget items include most spending, such as defense spending, where there is no specific dedicated tax revenue. Currently, most federal spending is classified as on-budget, with the exception of Social Security and the U.S. Post Office, which are classified as off-budget.

Off-budget items typically (but not always) have specific tax collections that are identified and designated to meet future outlays of the program. The rationale for having off-budget items is that the assets are segregated and, in theory, should be protected from being mingled with general on-budget operations. This makes a lot of sense, in theory. The practice of moving funds from off-budget to on-budget negates the intended benefit of segregation. The good news for politicians is that Congress can declare an item to be off-budget with the stroke of a pen. For example, when President Reagan purchased oil for the strategic oil reserve, those monies were declared off-budget, and as such, all spending for the oil reserve was not shown as spending. This accounting essentially allows the costs of a program to be removed from on-budget spending totals, even though the government is currently spending, or expects to spend, money on a program. The Office of Management and Budget has proposed combining on-budget and off-budget outlays, but to date, the proposed change has not been made.

Here is an example of how combining on-budget and off-budget spending can distort reality: At the end of his second term, President Clinton claimed that his administration had balanced the budget and created a surplus. To give President Clinton credit, he did manage to drive the deficit down to the lowest levels in recent times, but he did not balance the budget. Politicians and news people were so excited with the announcement that the country had a balanced budget that there was little if any investigation into whether the budget was truly balanced.

Let's dissect the on-budget/off-budget accounting gymnastics that occurred. The following table shows that the public debt was reduced by $363 billion from 1997 to 2000. It is also clear that, during this same period, the national debt increased by $261 billion. By logical examination, one of these numbers would seem to be wrong. In fact, they are both correct. It is just a matter of how the numbers are reported.

Year	Public Debt (Trillions)	National Debt (Trillions)
1997	$ 3.772	$ 5.413
1998	$ 3.721	$ 5.526
1999	$ 3.632	$ 5.656
2000	$ 3.409	$ 5.674

The national debt column shows an increase each year. If there were a surplus, the national debt number would have decreased, which it clearly did not. Either the U.S. Treasury reporting of national debt was incorrect or President Clinton never had a surplus. The latter is true. The public debt (debt borrowed from public sources that specifically excludes intergovernmental debt) did decrease, but the decrease was due to the movement of off-budget surpluses from the Social Security Trust Fund (SSTF) to on-budget accounts. This transfer reduced the amount the government needed to borrow from the public. Amounts borrowed from the SSTF are included in the national debt numbers but are not included in the public debt numbers, thus creating the appearance of a decrease in debt. This is why public debt should never be confused with or used in place of national debt. Public debt is approximately $7.8 trillion of the total national debt of $13 trillion.

Let's explore this accounting in more detail. During this same four-year period, off-budget agencies (predominantly Social Security) had surpluses amounting to $455 billion. Those amounts were transferred from the SSTF to fund on-budget operating accounts, thus giving the appearance that on-budget spending was less than it actually was. IOUs, in the form of Treasury securities, were issued to the SSTF for the surpluses that were transferred. The debt issued to the SSTF represents amounts that will eventually be paid to the Social Security recipients in the form of future benefit payments. The Clinton surplus was really nothing more than the transfer of excess off-budget surpluses to on-budget accounts.

The impact that on/off-budget surpluses has on the annual deficit numbers is clearly demonstrated in Table S-3 from the Office of Management and Budget (OMB) report dated May 2009. The report shows the projected on-budget/off-budget numbers by year, from 2010 to 2019.

Year 2010–2015	2010	2011	2012	2013	2014	2015
On-budget deficit	$1,405	$1,195	$933	$935	$986	$992
Off-budget surplus	$135	$152	$172	$192	$198	$195
On-budget deficit net of off-budget surplus	$1,270	$1,043	$761	$743	$788	$797

($ in billions)

Year 2016–2019	2016	2017	2018	2019	2010–2019
On-budget deficit	$1,108	$1,141	$1,162	$1,260	$11,117
Off-budget surplus	$201	$192	$185	$174	$1,794
On-budget deficit net of off-budget surplus	$907	$949	$977	$1,086	$9,323

($ in billions)

The number that will be shared most often with the public is the on-budget deficit amount reduced by the off-budget surplus. The cumulative total of the numbers from 2010 to 2019 is $9.323 trillion. However, the actual on-budget deficit is $11.117 trillion. The $1.794 trillion difference represents the IOUs that will be issued to off-budget accounts. That's like taking money from your wife's saving account and putting it into your savings account and then professing that your family net worth has increased. Nice try, but don't attempt to spend your "extra" money.

If all of these estimated numbers were to materialize, as projected, politicians would be talking about a $9.323 trillion deficit for this period, instead of the real number, which is $11.117 trillion.

It's like magic. The debt seems to mysteriously vanish, but it's all an illusion. It will reappear.

INTERGOVERNMENTAL DEBT IS REALLY PUBLIC DEBT

YOU CAN IGNORE IT, BUT IT IS NOT GOING AWAY.

Let's recap the way on-budget/off-budget spending is tracked and accounted for. The off-budget surpluses of the Social Security Trust Fund (SSTF) are transferred to on-budget accounts via Treasury IOUs. That transfer is recorded to an intergovernmental debt account. This intergovernmental debt account is not widely discussed and rarely mentioned. Just because intergovernmental debt is money that the government owes itself, that doesn't make the debt go away. This myth will expose itself when the SSTF starts to run at a deficit, which indicators point to occurring as early as 2011. When the government begins to repay the SSTF debt, it will also realize that intergovernmental debt is real, as the Treasury will have to issue additional public debt to fund the SSTF obligations.

Understanding how intergovernmental debt becomes public debt may be one of the most difficult government accounting concepts to follow. Intergovernmental debt is the debt that one governmental agency owes to another governmental agency. Public debt is debt that the government owes to anyone other than a governmental agency; that is, the public investor. The process by which intergovernmental debt becomes public debt really needs to be exposed for what it is—deception.

For decades, the nation's true debt picture has been distorted by excluding intergovernmental debt. Focus has been directed at the public debt, but it is the national debt (the combination of public debt and intergovernmental debt) that merits our concern. Let's examine why that is the case.

The following tables give a snapshot of on-budget spending, off-budget spending, public debt, intergovernmental debt, and national debt both at the governmental and household levels.

	On-Budget	Off-Budget
Governmental Level Examples	Essentially all spending except Social Security and the U.S. Post Office	The Social Security Trust Fund and the U.S. Post Office
Household Level Examples	Mortgage, car payments, and utility bills	College Trust Fund, 401K, IRA

	Definition	Example
Public Debt	Debt that the federal government owes to everyone else except for themselves	U.S. Treasury Bonds U.S. Savings Bonds
Intergovernmental Debt	Debt that one federal government agency owes to another federal agency	Notes and IOUs issued by the federal government; $2.7 trillion that have been taken from the SSTF and used by the general fund
National Debt	The combination of public and intergovernmental debt	

The Spender family wanted to buy a new house that was slightly more than they could currently afford. The father, Big Spender, had a good job and expected to receive future promotions and increases in salary. The anticipated pay increases would allow the family to afford the mortgage payment within the next few years, so they made the purchase. Big Spender just needed to bridge the gap for a couple of years until his pay raises materialized. To bridge the gap, Big Spender decided to borrow money from the college trust fund that his parents established to fund his twins' college educations. The borrowings would be just enough to cover the monthly mortgage payment short-fall. Every month, Big Spender would take money from the college fund to make the house payment, with the thought that it would be repaid once his raises kicked in. All was well, and the Spenders were living large.

Unfortunately his employer, Automotive Supplier, Inc., fell on hard times. Instead of receiving promotions and salary increases, Big Spender was asked to take a pay cut to help the company survive the downturn. Ever the optimist, Big Spender agreed to the reduction, knowing that he could borrow a little extra from the college fund each month to cover the family's mortgage. The situation turned from bad to worse when the downturn forced Automotive Supplier, Inc., out of business. Big Spender is now without a job. To make matters worse, the twins are now ready to go to college. Look at Big Spender's checkbook and the college trust fund account balances as he "borrows from Peter to pay Paul."

Big Spender's Checkbook				College Trust Fund		
Payment Number	Payment Amount	Income Amount	Balance (Shortfall)	With-drawal Number	Withdraw Amount (to pay mortgage shortfall)	Balance $1,400
1	$700	$500	($200)	1	($200)	$1,200
2	$700	$500	($200)	2	($200)	$1,000
3	$700	$400	($300)	3	($300)	$700
4	$700	$0	($700)	4	($700)	$0

The twins begin to focus on selecting colleges, but Big Spender is forced to tell them that he has depleted their college fund to make mortgage payments. If that wasn't bad enough, with the college fund now depleted, Big Spender can no longer use it as a source of funds. What will happen to the Spender family? They can no longer afford to pay the mortgage because the college fund that helped cover the monthly mortgage payment shortfall is depleted. Big Spender is faced with losing the family home, and the children are faced with no finances for their college education.

This example of fiscal irresponsibility is similar to ignoring intergovernmental debt. The mortgage payment represents the on-budget spending, while the college trust fund is analogous to the off-budget loans from the Social Security trust fund.

The Spender family example illustrates that when monies that have been set aside for specific use at a future date are borrowed against and not replaced, the obligation for which the monies were earmarked cannot be met. If the monies are not repaid, clearly there will be someone who will suffer. In our example it is the twins; in real life it will be those expecting government entitlements. The government would like us to believe that intergovernmental debt, the monies it owes to the SSTF, does not exist. The fact is that the SSTF monies have to be repaid in order to provide the future benefit. Because the government has failed to repay the borrowings from the SSTF, the government will not be capable of meeting the obligations of the SSTF without further borrowings or substantial tax increases.

In the story, everyone lost their future. That is what is on the horizon when the government can no longer tax the citizens of this country enough to pay the benefits and obligations it has promised.

The following example shows how money is currently moved between the on-budget/off-budget accounts and public and intergovernmental debt accounts. The numbers are in dollars, for illustration purposes, and are not specific to any particular period or budget. The only objective of the example is to show how the process works and how the corresponding numbers are reported.

On-Budget Accounts (Current Spending):

Year	Revenue	Outlays	Surplus (Deficit)
1	$1,000	$1,250	($250)
2	$1,200	$1,400	($200)
3	$1,300	$1,500	($200)

Summary for on-budget accounts:

Sub-total on-budget spending for years 1–3   ($650)

Loan from off-budget account SSTF $105 ←

Year 3 account balance—Public Debt   ($545)

Off-Budget Accounts (SSTF):

Year	Revenue	Outlays	Surplus (Deficit)
1	$200	$180	$20
2	$225	$190	$35
3	$250	$200	$50

Summary for off-budget accounts:

Sub-total off-budget collections for years 1–3 $105

Loan to on-budget account/Intergovernmental debt   ($105) ─┘

Year 3 SSTF account balance $0

Based on the example, the $105 is shifted from the off-budget accounts to the on-budget accounts, which results in reducing public debt. The government emphasis on the public debt of $545 is misleading when the debt is actually $650. The $105 needs to be repaid, as it was earmarked for a specific use at a later date. Failure to repay that money significantly impacts everyone down the line.

For the last forty years, on-budget spending (outlays) have exceeded revenues. This created the need to borrow money to fund the spending obligations. The U.S. Treasury borrows the money from two sources. The first source used to meet spending obligations is the issuing of public debt. The other source is the issuing of IOUs to the SSTF. As illustrated in this example, by the end of the third year, the cumulative on-budget deficit totaled $650. During this same period, Social Security (an off-budget account) generated a surplus of $105. Each year, the total Social Security surplus is loaned to the on-budget accounts. At the end of the third year, the national debt picture is:

Public Debt	$545
Intergovernmental Debt	<u>$105</u>
Total National Debt	$650

The total national debt at the end of year three is $650, which is the same number as the cumulative on-budget deficit for the period. Without the borrowing from the SSTF, the public debt would also be $650. Since the SSTF generated a $105 surplus; the government had to borrow $545 from the public to cover the on-budget deficit spending. Any way that you look at it, the debt is $650.

Next is the accounting for year four when SSTF outlays exceed revenue:

On-Budget Accounts (Current Spending):

Year	Revenue	Outlays	Surplus (Deficit)
4	$1,500	$1,500	$0

Off-budget Accounts (Social Security Account):

Year	Revenue	Outlays	Surplus (Deficit)
4	$250	$400	($150)

In year four, on-budget spending is equal to revenue, resulting in a deficit of $0 for the year. At the same time, the outlays for Social Security have accelerated and now exceed revenue, resulting in a $150 deficit. The on-budget account will need to repay the IOUs it has issued to the SSTF so that the SSTF can pay its obligations. To accomplish this, the government must either reduce on-budget spending to cover the IOUs or borrow $150 from the public to cover the year four off-budget deficit. This is how intergovernmental debt becomes public debt.

During the first three years, the SSTF shifted its excess funds to on-budget accounts, which is required by law. The SSTF did receive IOUs in the form of U.S. Treasury obligations for the funds transferred. In year four, the SSTF will have to call in the $150 worth of IOUs to meet their obligations of $150.

At the end of year four, the national debt comprises the following:

Public Debt at the end of year 3	$545
On-budget deficit year 4	$ 0
Off-budget deficit year 4	$150
Public Debt at the end of year 4	$695

As a result, the total national debt is:

Public Debt	$695
Intergovernmental Debt	$ 0
Total National Debt	$695

Once the SSTF starts to run at a deficit, the intergovernmental debt will become public debt. The fallacious argument that the government owes the money to itself will be exposed.

Since its inception, the SSTF has collected in excess of $2.7 trillion more than it has paid out. There are *zero dollars* in the SSTF, as *all* of the excess has been loaned to on-budget programs. When SSTF revenues (Social Security taxes) are less than the SSTF outlays (Social Security payments), the government will be forced to pay the IOUs back to the SSTF.

Going back to the Spender family example, when Big Spender was no longer able to borrow from the college trust fund, his irresponsibility jeopardized his family's future, and they faced financial ruin. The same is true for the government. Allowing millions of baby boomers to have a false sense of security is nothing short of total fiscal irresponsibility. When the government is no longer able to borrow from the SSTF, our nation's real level of debt will become apparent.

Intergovernmental debt can be ignored, but it's not going away.

WHERE DOES THE MONEY GO?
OUR NATION HAS A SPENDING PROBLEM!

If Congress fails to address spending and chooses instead to implement short-term solutions, spending will increase from its thirty-year historical average of 20.6 percent of GDP to nearly 25 percent of GDP in the next sixty years. In today's dollars, this equates to an increase of over $600 billion, or nearly 25 percent of the total revenue collections. While this may sound like a long time away, remember that Social Security is seventy-four years old and Medicare is just over forty years old. When dealing with numbers of this magnitude, a long-term approach must be developed, implemented, and maintained.

At the highest level, federal spending can be grouped into three basic categories: mandatory spending, discretionary spending, and net interest expense. For 2008, the spending by category and amount (in billions/1,000 billions=1 trillion) are as follows:

	Dollar Amount	Percentage
Mandatory Spending	$1,595	54%
Discretionary Spending	$1,135	38%
Net Interest Expense	$253	8%

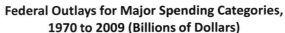
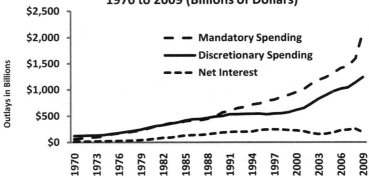

Federal Outlays for Major Spending Categories, 1970 to 2009 (Billions of Dollars)

CBO Historical Table F-5 Revised 1/24/10
http://www.cbo.gov/budget/historical.shtml

We will provide more background on all three types of spending, but our primary focus will be on mandatory programs, as they are the programs that place the nation's economy in highest peril. These programs are on the verge of creating an explosion of spending and, as a consequence, a skyrocketing debt. Discretionary spending is largely driven by outlays for national defense. Defense spending will eventually decline by about $100 billion per year if, and when, the global war on terrorism (GWOT) is scaled down. Net interest expense is the interest paid on our national debt. The only way to control net interest expense is to operate at a surplus and pay down the national debt.

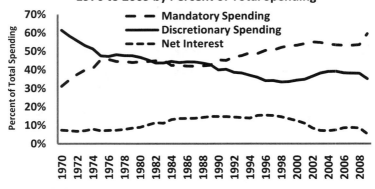

Federal Outlays for Major Spending Categories, 1970 to 2009 by Percent of Total Spending

CBO Historical Table F-5 Revised 1/24/10
http://www.cbo.gov/budget/historical.shtml

MANDATORY SPENDING

Mandatory outlays, sometimes referred to as direct spending, are usually authorized by permanent laws. Mandatory outlays primarily consist of entitlement programs such as Social Security, Medicare, and Medicaid. The level of the outlay is dictated by the number of recipients enrolled in the program, not the dollar amount of the outlay. Thus, as the number of participants increases, the amount of the outlay will automatically increase, absent a change in law.

Mandatory program outlays have increased from approximately 30 percent in 1962 to over 50 percent today. Mandatory outlays will continue to escalate due to an aging population unless changes in policy are implemented to stem the growth. The Congressional Budget Office (CBO) has estimated that by 2080, absent changes, outlays on just the Medicare and Medicaid entitlements will eclipse the amount the government spends today on all programs.

With the costs of mandatory entitlement programs increasing due to an aging population as well as the increase in health-care costs, it is easy to understand why the president is attempting to address this issue. Solving the escalating mandatory spending problem will be neither quick nor easy. As addressed earlier, Congress cannot solve the problem with only a tax increase. Someone is going to have to foot the bill, be it the taxpayer in the form of radical tax changes, the user in the form of reduced benefits, or a combination of the two. Continuing to operate as we do today is not an option the nation can afford.

DISCRETIONARY SPENDING

Discretionary spending encompasses the programs that Congress approves on an annual basis. The amounts vary, or at least should, depending on revenue and expenditure requirements. Defense spending is the largest single discretionary item. It has averaged 4.5 percent of GDP over the last thirty years.

Arguably, protection of its citizens and their property is one of the primary duties of a government. There will always be some level of defense spending. In 2008, defense spending was $616 billion, or 54 percent of total discretionary spending and approximately 20 percent of total spending. That $616 billion spent on defense includes approximately $100 billion to fund the global war on terrorism (GWOT). As the financial demands resulting from the GWOT diminish, the amount spent on defense in both absolute dollars and as a percent of GDP will diminish. Once that happens, those funds will be freed up to fund other obligations. Let's hope that happens sooner rather than later; our nation needs the money elsewhere.

NET INTEREST

Net interest expense is the interest that is paid on the public debt. Net interest expense specifically excludes the interest that is owed on intergovernmental debt. The issuing governmental agency treats the interest outlay as expenditure. The receiving governmental agency treats the interest receipt as income. Since both are governmental agencies, the paying and receiving of monies offset each other. The argument is that since both expense and income are within the same set of books, it is proper to net the two. This does sound reasonable, except, as discussed earlier, intergovernmental debt eventually will become public debt. The interest is not owed to the government. It is owed to the retirees who are participating in Social Security and other entitlement programs. When the benefits are ultimately paid to the Social Security Trust Fund (SSTF), the IOUs will have to be redeemed. Recall what happened to Big Spender and his family. The result will be that the government will have to issue public debt to fund the obligation. At that point, the debt shifts from intergovernmental to public debt and net interest expense will approach gross interest expense.

In 2008, gross interest was $451 billion and the net interest was $253 billion. Interest owed to the SSTF, other trust funds, and monies collected from investments was $198 billion for the year. Essentially, this process allows the government to totally ignore interest expense owed to other governmental agencies. It has to be repaid, yet as a nation we do not seem to be overly concerned.

It is projected that 2010 net interest expense, as a percent of GDP, will be at the lowest level in over forty years, yet the national debt is at its highest level ever. Where's the disconnect? The fact that net interest expense is at a recent low is not due to any action of Congress but is strictly a function of market interest rates. When interest rates rise, and they will, the combination of the record debt and higher interest rates will result in a rapid escalation of our nation's interest expense. To offset this increase, financial resources will have to be diverted from other on-budget programs or our nation will have to increase its level of borrowing. This only further increases the national debt crisis.

In addition to interest rate changes, the government must also be concerned with the average length of maturity (duration) of its debt. Under the Clinton administration, it was decided to reduce the length of maturity on government issued IOUs (borrowings) to take advantage of lower short-term interest rates. That means the government will need to reissue its IOUs on a more frequent basis, making their interest rates more susceptible to changes. This is similar to home owners who took adjustable rate mortgages to finance their homes. When interest rates increased they could not make their house payments.

Today the average interest rate on government debt is 3.3 percent. In January 2008, the average rate was 4.8 percent; a full 1.5 percent higher. On $12 trillion, the increase in interest rates would result in an increase in annual interest expense of $180 billion.

By now it should be apparent that the annual deficit is the result of escalating spending. It is the mounting annual deficits that are driving the national debt higher. Simply stated, the more we spend, the more we need to tax or the annual deficit will rise. Control and or lower spending and the deficit will go down without raising taxes.

Where did the money go? Our government spent it and more. Our nation really has a spending problem! To rephrase a presidential election sound bite, "It's not the economy; it's the spending, stupid!"

SOCIAL SECURITY TRUST FUND

THE GOOD NEWS IS THAT THE SSTF HAS $2.7 TRILLION. THE BAD NEWS IS IT IS INVESTED IN GOVERNMENT IOUS.

The Federal Old Age and Survivors Insurance and Federal Disability Insurance Trust Funds (OASDI), better known as Social Security Trust Funds (SSTF), came into existence in August of 1935, when President Roosevelt signed the Social Security Act into law. The objective of the plan was to provide assistance to citizens in their twilight years. Over the years, the plan has evolved into what many rely on as their only form of retirement income. At the end of 2008, approximately fifty-one million people were drawing from the SSTF. When a retired individual receives his/her Social Security check, it is *not a gift* from the government; it is actually a *return* of funds that the recipient and his/her employer have equally paid into the fund over the employee's working life.

Over the years, the Social Security program has been modified and expanded well beyond its original intent. According to the SSTF Trustees Report, since its inception, Social Security has amassed an unfunded liability of nearly $6.6 trillion. This means that using current assumptions, Social Security is projected to pay $7 trillion more in benefits than it has collected or expects to collect.

What changes have been made? In 1939, amendments were made to include payments to widows and their minor children. In 1950, amendments were made to expand eligibility and increased the number of workers covered by ten million. The amendments also increased benefit levels, which had been essentially constant since the inception of the program. This resulted in an immediate benefit increase of 77 percent and a corresponding 77 percent increase in outlays. Amendments in 1954 and 1956 expanded disability coverage to workers and disabled adult children. In 1961, the age at which a male could participate was lowered to sixty-two. Other changes included the passage of Medicare, which remained under the Social Security umbrella until 1977, at which time it became the responsibility of Health Care Financing Administration, later renamed the Center for Medicare and Medicaid Services. In 1972, Congress enacted automatic cost of living adjustments (COLAs) to increase benefits for the impact of inflation and created Supplemental Security Income (SSI). Since then, changes in administration, services, and benefits have been made. The reason to review these changes in the program is not to provide a comprehensive historical overview, as there have been many other changes we have not discussed. The reviewed changes demonstrate that *any* program, regardless of its original intent, will, over time, suffer from changes to its scope. This generally results in increased costs. Based on recent statements by the Social Security trustees, it should be clear that Social Security, as it exists today, cannot be sustained. It is a certainty that program costs will increase dramatically over the next ten years, as the baby-boomer generation enters the program. If you don't believe there really is a problem, you only need to read the disclaimer that is included on page 2 of your most recent Social Security Statement:

> The law governing benefit amounts may change because, by 2041, the payroll taxes collected will be enough to pay only about 78 percent of the scheduled benefits.

By 2041, most baby boomers will have passed through the system. The question is what will be left in the SSTF? This should be a wake-up call for all those still working and paying into the SSTF. The 2009 Annual SSTF Trustees Report is even more ominous, predicting that benefits will be reduced to 75 percent by 2037 versus the 2041 projection just one year ago. The statement by the trustees is basically an admission that the actuarial projections for the revenue collected, the level of benefits paid, and the participation levels are inadequate. Keeping an eye out for the 2010 Trustees Report is a good idea. The report will be published around the middle of May 2010. It can be found at http://www.ssa.gov/OACT/TRSUM/index.html. All indications point to these numbers deteriorating further by the time the report is published.

What started as a 1 percent tax on the first $3,000 of income in 1937 has escalated to a 6.2 percent tax (12.4 percent including the employer portion) on an inflation-indexed wage base. This means that the base earnings amount that is subject to Social Security tax will automatically increase every year. Even though both rates and tax base have steadily escalated, the program is in trouble. As noted earlier, it is highly probable that the program may not be able to pay current benefit levels to beneficiaries as they become eligible to participate in the plan. When Social Security was implemented, the life expectancy for men was sixty and for women sixty-four. Today, the life expectancy for men is seventy-five and for women eighty. Life expectancy numbers should continue to rise, which extends the duration of the payout. This increased longevity of the population will place even more strain on the system. The history of Social Security rates and income bases can be found in the appendix.

Let's discuss a few fundamental facts about Social Security. First and foremost, there is *no* actual money in the SSTF. There is an account, somewhere on the government's ledger, called the SSTF, but it does not have *any* money in it. The balance is absolutely zero. What the fund does have is IOUs in the form of Treasury securities. These IOUs amount to approximately $2.7 trillion. The IOUs represent the monies that SSTF has loaned to other governmental agencies to fund on-budget expenditures over the past decades. Let's be very clear on this point. Since its inception, the taxes paid into SSTF by employees and employers have exceeded the amount paid to recipients by approximately $2.7 trillion, yet the plan is underfunded by nearly $7 trillion.

Based on current participation and contribution levels, the program cannot continue to run at the surplus levels it once did. The number of participants paying into the plan is shrinking in relation to those receiving benefits. In 1945, there were nearly forty-two workers paying into the system for every beneficiary. By 1975, that ratio had decreased to 3.2 workers paying for every beneficiary. That is where it stands today. Based on economic assumptions published by various governmental agencies, that number will continue to decline to 2.5 workers per recipient by 2025. Based on the CBO summer 2009 baseline, 2.5

93

workers per Social Security recipient will result in an average $430 monthly shortfall for each Social Security recipient.

The changes in life expectancy and payout ratios will also have a very significant impact on the long-term viability of the program. To demonstrate the impact, we developed a simple model using the Social Security tax rate and income base information to show the amount of taxes paid and the expected payout for an individual who exited college, worked for forty-four years, and retired at age sixty-six. For simplicity, assume that the individual paid the maximum into the plan every year and reached their actuarial life expectancy. The model shows that Social Security would pay out nearly $118,000 more than this hypothetical individual paid in SS taxes. And this is not an anomaly. A review of statements for individuals earning $30,000 per year shows that their payout exceeds the taxes paid as well. The only way this math works, all other things being equal, is to increase the number of individuals paying into the system and increase the tax rate that individuals pay or curtail benefit levels. The option of discontinuing or greatly reducing Social Security payments would be extremely unpopular.

Taxes employee paid over work life	$110,806
Taxes employer paid over work life	$110,806
Total SS taxes paid	$221,612
Projected monthly benefit	$2,300
Life expectancy in years	78.3
Years in retirement (78.3-66)	12.3
Number of months in retirement	147.6
Expected payout	$339,480
Shortfall	($117,867.62)

The latest report from the Social Security and Medicare Board of Trustees (BOT) highlights the magnitude of the problem. To fund the SSTF for the future, the BOT estimates that an immediate 16 percent payroll tax increase (from 12.4 percent to 14.4 percent) would be required to solidify the future of the program. The May 2009 OMB report (Table S-4) shows that the SSTF will begin running a deficit in 2015. From 2015 to 2019 the fund will have a cumulative projected deficit of $225 billion. Current projections estimate that the fund will begin running a deficit by 2011 or 2012.

You could look at the accounting that the government is using for Social Security and conclude that it's the largest Ponzi scheme known to man, and you would be right. However, since it's a government plan they call it government accounting.

Social Security outlays are driven by participation level. Looking at the expected growth in participation levels from 2000 to 2045 only serves to reinforce the solvency risks the SSTF faces. In 2000, the United States had a population of 281 million people, of which approximately 35 million, or 12 percent, were over sixty-five years old. By 2030, the U.S. Bureau of the Census expects that slightly more than 81 million people will be over age sixty-five. The Social Security Trustees Report states that there will be 70.8 million people over age sixty-five. The variance of ten million people between the two agencies is 14 percent. If SSTF trustees are wrong and the census number is correct, the SSTF numbers only get worse. It doesn't matter which number is correct; it will still be a massive increase.

The following charts are based on the SSTF Trustees Report. They show how the over-sixty-five population is expected to grow from 1950 to 2080.

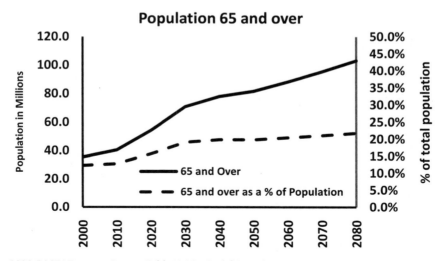

2009 OASDI Trustees Report Table V.A2.- Social Security Area Population as of July 1, 2009

Population Percentage Breakdown

- ■ 65 and over as a % of Population
- ■ Under 20 as a Percent of Population
- ■ 20-64 as a Percent of Population

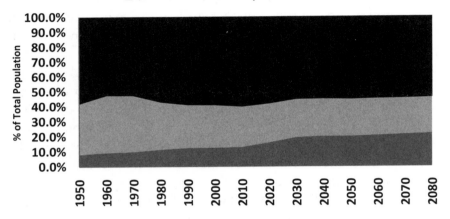

2009 OASDI Trustees Report Table V.A2.- Social Security
Area Population as of July 1, 2009

Year Over Year Change in Population

- ----- Growth of 65 and older
- — — Growth of Under 20
- —— Growth of 20-64

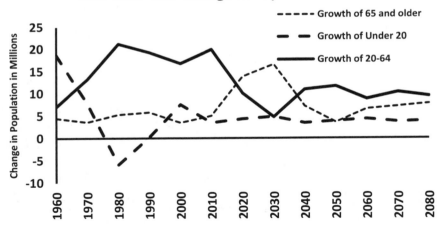

2009 OASDI Trustees Report Table V.A2.- Social Security
Area Population as of July 1, 2009

We had all better hope that the government can make good on the IOUs it owes to the Social Security Trust Fund (SSTF).

MEDICARE

IT IS IN VERY POOR HEALTH.
DON'T CALL THE DOCTOR, BECAUSE WE CAN'T AFFORD ONE.

The following chart is from the 2009 Annual Report of the Board of Trustees of the Federal Old Age and Survivors Insurance and Federal Disability Insurance Trust Funds. It illustrates the current spending and revenue trends for Medicare (HI) based on current trends and projections. The chart shows that HI costs should exceed revenues in the 2009–2010 timeframe and continue to increase thereafter to in excess of 13 percent of payroll from today's 2.9 percent level.

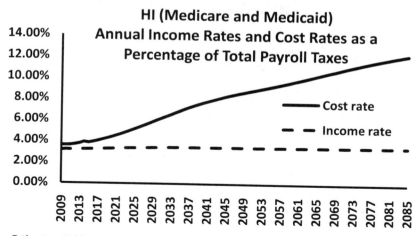

Estimates   Table VI.F2.- OASDI and HI Annual Income Rates, Cost Rates, and Balances using itermediate assumptions
http://www.ssa.gov/OACT/TR/TR05/lr6F2-3.html

Congress has steadily increased Medicare taxes since 1966 in an effort to cover the rising costs of the program. In the first year of the program, the combined employee/employer tax rate was 0.7 percent on the first $6,600 of income. Today the combined rate is 2.9 percent on an unlimited income base.

In 1945, President Truman asked Congress to pass legislation for a national health insurance plan. Congress had an ongoing debate on the issue for twenty years. In 1965, President Johnson signed Medicare and Medicaid into law as part of his "Great Society" program. At the time, America was in its industrial prime and many believed that the growth trends required to fund the future costs of the programs would continue. History, as it often does, proved them wrong. While the economy did continue to grow, the rate of growth slowed substantially. The following chart shows the growth in GDP from 1960 to 2015.

Yearly Growth Rate of U.S. GDP

* Estimate   Table 1.2—SUMMARY OF RECEIPTS, OUTLAYS, AND SURPLUSES OR DEFICITS (–) AS PERCENTAGES OF GDP: 1930–2015
http://www.whitehouse.gov/omb/budget/Historicals/

As indicated, the GDP growth rate peaked in the late '70s. The trend line indicates that GDP rate of growth has continued to decline every decade since. The economic growth rates that supported the initial financial projections have continued to decline, which has resulted in reductions in plan revenues. Because the growth has slowed, Congress has resorted to HI tax rate increases and an escalation of the income base to maintain solvency.

According to the report, the Medicare and Medicaid programs have an actuarial unfunded liability of $36.6 trillion. Yes, $36.6 trillion. That amounts to an annual unfunded liability of $840 billion per year since the program's inception. The ability of the government to accurately project cost must be questioned. Care needs to be taken to identify the source of the variances. The variances lie not with the forecasters but with the assumptions that the forecasters are given. The assumptions are generally promoted by the representatives supporting the legislation. If the numbers don't work, they change the assumptions until they do. When we end up with a major shortfall like we have with Medicare and Medicaid, no one will recall what assumptions were even used. If the HI program were required to be fully funded, it would have bankrupted the nation years ago. Rather than address the issue, our leaders have chosen to ignore and defer the problem to the point where the program has placed the economy of the entire nation in peril.

The first paragraph, "Message to the Public," of the Trustees Report offers a succinct overview of the challenges the program faces.

> The financial condition of the Social Security and Medicare programs remains challenging. Projected long run program costs are not sustainable under current program parameters. ... Medicare's financial status is much worse. As was true in 2008, Medicare's Hospital Insurance (HI) Trust Fund is expected to pay out more in hospital benefits and other expenditures this year than it receives in taxes and other dedicated revenues. The difference will be made up by redeeming trust fund assets. Growing annual deficits are projected to exhaust HI reserves in 2017, after which the percentage of scheduled benefits payable from tax income would decline from 81 percent in 2017 to about 50 percent in 2035 and 30 percent in 2080. In addition, the Medicare Supplementary Medical Insurance (SMI) Trust Fund that pays for physician services and the prescription drug benefit will continue to require general revenue financing and charges on beneficiaries

that grow substantially faster than the economy and beneficiary incomes over time.

While the message is intended for the general public, it is doubtful that the general public has read or even heard any portion of the report; that's very unfortunate. What is clear, through the endorsement by the trustees, is that this program is simply not sustainable. The trustees are Timothy F. Geithner, secretary of the Treasury; Kathleen Sebelius, secretary of health and human Services; Hilda L. Solis, secretary of labor; and Michael J. Astrue, commissioner of Social Security. This group can hardly be considered conservative, so it cannot be argued that this is some ultra-conservative group out to make a political point. The only point that can be made is that our nation is facing a wave of debt looming in the not-too-distant future.

In 2008, Medicare spent approximately $468 billion in benefits as compared to $425 billion in benefits in 2007. Forty-five million participants were covered in 2008, an increase of one million from the previous year. When the program was implemented, payroll taxes were intended to cover the costs of the programs. That worked as long as the number of people paying into the plan was adequate to cover the participants receiving benefits. With a program that is already stressed, the addition of baby boomers will only exacerbate the problem. It is this inclusion that is driving the trend displayed in the chart shown earlier.

The 2009 report estimates that the HI Trust Fund assets will be exhausted by 2017, two years earlier than projected in the 2008 report. This is not a new phenomenon. The trustees have not considered the program to be satisfactory since 2003.

Plan costs are expected to increase from the current level of 1.6 percent of GDP to 5 percent of GDP in 2083. This may not sound like much, but tax collections are historically 18.3 percent of GDP. Therefore, in 2083, HI costs are expected to consume 27 percent of all taxes collected. The costs for Medicare Part B currently average 1.3 percent of GDP and are expected to increase to 4.5 percent by 2083. During this same period, it is estimated that outlays for Medicare Part D will increase from the current level of 0.4 percent of GDP to nearly 2 percent. While B and D have separate trust funds and sources of revenue, their future is as uncertain as HI. As general funds are shifted to cover B and D expenses, on-budget programs will face offsetting funding reductions.

So what went wrong? In 1966, when the plan was implemented, the projections that led to a 0.7 percent tax on $6,600 were either grossly miscalculated or the projections were engineered to support passage of the plan without regard to the future. Regardless, taxpayers will be paying for that decision for the next seventy years.

As the health-care debate continues and costs skyrocket, it seems that the only ones who understand the ramifications of passing additional legislation are those that will have to pay for it.

This program may be terminally ill.

IT'S TIME TO SINK OR SWIM

WE HAVE THE ABILITY TO STAY AFLOAT, BUT IT WILL REQUIRE CHANGE AND SACRIFICE.

We took on writing this book to share facts about our country's economic crisis, not to advance a political ideological position. It is our hope that we articulated the facts in a way that will allow you to use them to formulate your own opinions.

We wanted to hold our opinions and suggestions for addressing the economic crisis until the end, and here we are. Let's begin with the premise that the country's current economic problems and the ones just around the corner are huge. Projections of the unfunded liabilities, which do not include the current debt of $13 trillion, range from $50 trillion to $107 trillion. While there are many reasons that estimates can be so far apart, there is little need to be exact or debate the magnitude of the nation's financial quandary. Be it $50 trillion or $107 trillion, it's still a big number.

While a balanced budget sounds good, up to now it has just been rhetoric. A balanced budget is not projected for at least the next ten years and most likely a lot longer. Balancing the budget today would take spending reductions, revenue increases, or some combination that would amount to hundreds of billions of dollars. The latest projections for 2010 have the deficit reaching $1.5 trillion. On their own, dramatic tax increases wouldn't come close to eliminating the budget deficit. The Bush-era tax cuts, if allowed to expire at the end of 2010, will have minimal impact on revenue. It would take a 30 percent increase in taxes to generate an extra $1 trillion in tax revenue. That would equate to a nearly 100 percent increase of the current tax rate structure. A tax increase of that size would surely dampen the economy. If we cut spending across the board by 25 percent, it would also generate about $1 trillion in savings. That means cutting funding for airport security, education, defense, unemployment insurance, veteran's benefits, Social Security, Medicare, and every other program the government funds by 25 percent. Reducing funding for all of these programs would be extremely unpopular with voters. Reality tells us that some programs are more important than others in terms of economic growth and the safety of the nation. Smaller or no cuts to some programs only mean that the others will have to be cut more. This option is equally unrealistic.

Now that the facts are clearer, some may believe that there is no way out of this dilemma. Frankly, that may be true unless there are substantial and sustained changes on several fronts. Is there an easy solution or quick fix? NO! Are there solutions? Yes, but no solution will be quick, easy, painless or free. The economic problems are not insurmountable but they need to be addressed soon with sustainable actions.

It is not realistic to think that the federal government can be all things to all people. Difficult decisions need to be made on what programs the federal government should continue as well as the appropriate levels of funding for those deemed essential. The national debt has been growing for over forty years. We are not going to eradicate the national debt in ten or even twenty years.

We cannot rely on the media or politicians to define economic progress. Their motives should be suspect, as the media is selling advertising and the politicians are selling themselves to voters. Some aspects of the economy will improve, while others will deteriorate. This is how an economy works. Improving economic indicators (rising employment, auto starts increasing to fifteen million units per year, housing starts growing to an annual rate of one million units, factory orders increasing for the sixth straight month, or the balance of trade slowing) do not necessarily mean that the economy is getting better or worse. They only mean that a particular metric or segment of the economy is getting better or worse. At some point over the last forty years, each of these indicators had shown positive trends, yet the national debt continued to increase. A single indicator does not indicate a sound economy. Can we have economic prosperity in the private sector while the government continues to pile up debt? The answer is no. We need only to look at the economic situations in Greece, Japan, and Britain to understand that countries can go broke, and the United States is no exception. It would be hard to convince anyone that we had achieved economic prosperity just because the unemployment rate stood at 3 percent if the national debt continues to grow by $1 trillion per year. Lawrence Summers, President Obama's economic adviser, before entering government asked, "How long can the world's biggest borrower remain the world's biggest power?" His question was both insightful and thought provoking.

Before we start exploring solutions, let's briefly review the significant facts presented in this book:

> Our nation has been on a journey of fiscal irresponsibility that resulted in the national debt rising every year for the last forty years.
> 54.6 percent of all taxes are paid by 4.7 percent of the taxpayers, and 70 percent of all taxes are paid by 10 percent of the taxpayers.
> Mandatory spending now accounts for 57 percent of all spending and will continue to escalate as baby boomers become eligible for entitlement programs. Social Security has an unfunded liability of $6.6 trillion, and Medicare has an unfunded liability of $36.4 trillion (before passage of the health-care plan).
> On-budget and off-budget accounts have been comingled and distort the level of spending. The national debt is trending toward $13 trillion and is expected to increase by an average of $800 billion per year for the next ten years.

While this list is not all encompassing, it represents significant items that must be addressed if our nation is going to avoid the financial tsunami. Should we continue down our current path, it will be impossible to establish financial prosperity and the tsunami will crash down upon us.

Fiscal irresponsibility is the result of spending too much, taxing too little, or a combination of the two. Fiscal responsibility can only be achieved by reaching a balance between taxes and spending. Taxes can't go to 100 percent and spending cannot go to zero, so balance is required. The problems we face today are the result of a prolonged and growing imbalance. If spending continues to escalate and the national debt continues to rise, the economy will eventually contract, resulting in another recession or even a depression. Likewise, if legislators attempt to increase taxes to a level necessary to cover the government's voracious spending appetite, the nation's economy will be subject to a similar fate. What has been apparent for the last forty years is that the revenues collected have not been adequate to cover the level of spending. Collecting $2.7 trillion and spending $3.5 trillion cannot go on indefinitely. So what can be done?

We have identified several steps that should be taken that would put our nation back on the path toward fiscal responsibility. While the list is not exhaustive, if these simple suggestions are implemented, our nation will move toward being fiscally responsible while minimizing the impact on all citizens.

Those steps are:

➢ Change the tax laws
➢ Modify entitlement program spending
➢ Deal with real numbers
➢ Impose term limits
➢ Make your vote count

CHANGE THE TAX LAWS

Establish a tax base that will allow funding of current programs and extinguishment of debt.

Tax increases may ultimately be necessary but should only be done when it is clear that Congress has systematically evaluated all other alternatives. While advocating revenue increases may sound like heresy, revising the tax code could increase revenues without increasing the cost to taxpayers. Can revenue increases really be accomplished without increasing taxpayer costs? Yes. On the surface, that may not seem plausible, but here's how it could happen.

The U.S. Department of Treasury estimates that the voluntary compliance rate for taxpayers is approximately 84 percent. The remaining 16 percent is called the "tax gap" and represents amounts that are underreported, underpaid, or simply not filed. According to 2001 numbers, the most current data published by the Treasury, the tax gap by category is:

Underreporting	$285 billion
Underpayment	$33 billion
Non-filing	$27 billion

The current tax system is not able to close this gap without significant costs and intrusion into the personal lives of taxpayers. A major tax system revision that enables the Treasury to capture a significant portion of the tax gap would result in the collection of several hundred billion dollars of revenue. Due to the age of the information, the estimates most likely understate the potential benefit.

Changing the tax code could have other benefits in addition to closing the tax gap. There is the potential to also reduce the cost of tax compliance. The cost of compliance represents the cost that the government, individuals, and corporations spend on filing and collecting tax revenue. The cost of tax compliance is estimated to be in the range of $200 to $300 billion per year. Implementing a simpler tax code that minimizes reporting requirements on the part of taxpayers and greatly reduces the need for the government to oversee collections would result in significant savings. If the government could capture a portion of the savings associated with compliance, it would increase revenue without increasing the overall costs to taxpayers. Changing the tax code to a simpler system would allow the government to capture the combined benefits of compliance changes and the tax gap. This could generate hundreds of billions of dollars in revenue.

Over the last fifteen years, many books have been written on the benefits of the fair tax, flat tax, and similar programs (actually Milton Friedman proposed this in the '60s). While all approach the issue from slightly different paths, they are all directed toward a simpler and more equitable tax system that would capture a large portion of the tax gap and reduce the cost of compliance. While a study to overhaul the tax code is beyond the scope of this book, it is clear that the current system is inadequate and needs to be studied by experts. The study should identify the amount necessary to fund current obligations and also include the amount it would take to shrink the national debt. Clearly this will require a long-term approach and will require politicians to evaluate the merits of current programs and determine which ones will survive and in what form. With an expanding population base drawing from the programs and a declining GDP, it is mathematically impossible for all programs to survive in their current form.

MODIFY ENTITLEMENT PROGRAM SPENDING

Match revenue streams and determine the level of GDP that will be spent on entitlement programs.

Our leaders must stop ignoring the $43 trillion unfunded liabilities that have been disclosed in Social Security and Medicare Trustees Reports. This problem is not going to go away by itself, nor is it going to go away without some level of pain on the part of the recipients. These reports identify the exposure of the entitlement programs, yet our nation's leaders have failed to address the issues for fear of losing votes. Changes to entitlement programs are going to result in reductions in benefits at several levels. The Trustees Reports say that in very clear and specific terms. Seventy or 80 percent of a benefit is better than 100 percent of nothing.

An individual whose monthly bills total $6,700 and who has monthly income of $225 would be quick to make changes in his/her spending habits. These proportionately represent the budget numbers our nation currently faces. The government cannot pretend that there is not a problem just because payments have not or are not due to be made. Anyone who has had a college loan knows that this liability that would need to be funded (paid) in the future. Would we expect our children to pay our college loans? Congress is going to have to take responsibility for fiscally managing the spending programs it has passed and not continue to pass the buck to future generations of taxpayers.

Today, spending on Social Security, Medicare, and Medicaid is nearly $1.4 trillion annually. By 2020, that number is expected to approach $2.7 trillion (approximately the current revenue number). With the revised estimates of Obama-care increasing by $150 billion just weeks after passage of the bill, it's a good bet that the costs for that program will result in additional spending. A solution that considers a systematic yearly reduction of benefit levels over the next twenty years for those entering these programs should be considered. This would allow future participants adequate time to adjust their retirement plans to account for a reduced benefit level. Freezing current benefit levels for a period of time and scaling back future increases for inflation are additional options that should be explored. Many options exist, yet nothing is being done to contain or reduce costs. The current reports indicate that benefit levels are going to have to decrease. Why are our leaders waiting to make a change?

Our nation cannot ignore its social responsibilities in the process of balancing the budget. The key is determining the greatest need and prioritizing what is truly important and funding those priorities to the fullest extent. For years, our political leaders have used social programs to secure votes. Any effort to determine which programs should not be funded will be met with resistance. The loss and/or reduction of social programs are what people in Greece are currently rioting over. Will violence and destruction of property change the fact that Greece is bankrupt and can no longer afford these programs? Many of our own states are finding that they can no longer afford all of the social programs currently in place.

A theory attributed to Alexander Tytler, a Scottish lawyer, historian, and writer, sums up the dilemma: "A democracy cannot exist as a permanent form of government. It can only exist until the majority discovers it can vote itself largess out of the public treasury. After that, the majority always votes for the candidate promising the most benefits with the result the democracy collapses because of the loose fiscal policy ensuing, always to be followed by a dictatorship, then a monarchy."

Determining which programs to fund will not be easy, but the longer we delay, the greater the chance, like in Greece, that the decisions may be made for us.

DEAL WITH REAL NUMBERS

Our government needs to deal with real numbers. Legislators need to face the facts if they want to develop a cohesive plan to avoid the financial tsunami. They need to provide realistic and honest assumptions to the CBO when proposing legislation. Better still, they should have to identify and allocate the sources of revenue before a program begins to pay any benefits. That way, programs could be reexamined prior to the program start date and scaled accordingly based on outlays and revenue.

Borrowing from the Social Security Trust Fund (SSTF) or any other off-budget fund to pay for current obligations and calling it intergovernmental debt does not solve the problem and does not reflect reality. As discussed earlier, intergovernmental debt will eventually become public debt when the SSTF starts running at a deficit later this year or early next year. The option of continuing to fund on-budget expenditures with off-budget money is going to evaporate, as will the ability to mix on-budget and off-budget accounts. The new health-care legislation provides the government with a new source of intergovernmental debt, as it will collect revenues for four years before most benefits begin. Already, politicians that supported the bill point to how it will reduce the deficit. That may be initially true, but only until benefits begin to be paid. Such claims should now be transparent, as we know that it will have no effect on reducing the national debt.

IMPOSE TERM LIMITS

Arguably, the most difficult change that politicians must address is term limits. In the early '90s, the cry for term limits was a hot political topic with both the electorate and politicians. When some politicians reconciled themselves to the fact that they may have to join the American workforce and give up their elected office, their interest in term limits quickly waned. There is absolutely no doubt that the proliferation of career politicians has stymied governmental objectivity. The drive for reelection is exactly why all but a handful of politicians refuse to admit that there is a problem with Social Security and Medicare programs. They know that changing anything that impacts as many voters as these two programs is a recipe for losing a future election. To force politicians to focus on doing what is right for the country versus what is right for their reelection, both the Congress and the Senate should be limited to twelve years in office. Twelve years of making decisions that affect all Americans should be enough; in some cases, it may be more than enough. Political offices have evolved into job entitlements. Term limits have to be addressed if we are going to have politicians who will place the interest of the nation before their own self-interest.

MAKE YOUR VOTE COUNT

There is one more item to be considered, and it is arguably the most important. It has to do with the vote that each and every citizen casts when they step into the voting booth. Every vote is important. All of us must become better-informed voters, and those who have failed to vote in the past need to start casting their votes. We can no longer vote based on our ideological beliefs alone. A voter must consider the need to balance both social and fiscal responsibility. We cannot continue to allow the government to make promises in an effort to secure votes while mortgaging the future of the nation. We are mortgaged to the hilt. We have steadily marched down this path for forty years, and we now know where it leads. Having now been presented with the facts, there should be no question that what has been done has not worked.

On January 20, 1961, President John F. Kennedy said, "And so, my fellow Americans, ask not what your country can do for you—ask what you can do for your country." This excerpt from his inaugural speech may have more relevance today than it did then. In 1961 we had a military presence in Viet Nam, the threat of communism was ever present, and our national debt was about $2 billion. Nearly fifty years later, our country is still engaged in conflicts around the world, but our national debt is sixty-five hundred times larger.

We find ourselves in the midst of these economically perilous times because voters cast votes based on what they believed the country (i.e., the federal government) could do for them. If we as a nation are to survive this financial tsunami, voters must consider what is right for their country as a whole and not only what is right for themselves. It is the only way that we can pass on to future generations the United States of America as we know it.

Will we as a nation sink or swim? The choice is ours to make.

APPENDIXES

APPENDIX A: FEDERAL FINANCIAL STATISTICAL OVERVIEW

($$ in billions)	President Party	GDP	Revenue	Outlay	Excess (deficit)	Change in GDP	Revenue % to GDP	Public Debt Outsdg	Outlay % to GDP	Federal Debt Outsdg	Federal Debt Change	Federal Debt % Change
1934	D	$66	$3	$7	($4)		4.55%		10.61%	$27		
1935	D	$73	$4	$6	($2)	10.60%	5.48%		8.22%	$29	-$2	6.30%
1936	D	$84	$4	$8	($4)	15.10%	4.76%		9.52%	$34	-$5	17.40%
1937	D	$92	$5	$8	($3)	9.50%	5.43%		8.70%	$36	-$3	8.00%
1938	D	$86	$7	$7	$0	-6.50%	8.14%	$41	8.14%	$37	-$1	1.90%
1939	D	$92	$6	$9	($3)	7.00%	6.52%	$43	9.78%	$40	-$3	8.90%
1940	D	$101	$7	$9	($2)	9.80%	6.93%	$48	8.91%	$43	-$3	6.20%
1941	D	$127	$8	$14	($6)	25.70%	6.30%	$68	11.02%	$49	-$6	14.00%
1942	D	$162	$15	$35	($20)	27.60%	9.26%	$128	21.60%	$72	-$24	48.10%
1943	D	$199	$24	$79	($55)	22.80%	12.06%	$185	39.70%	$137	-$64	88.70%
1944	D	$220	$44	$91	($47)	10.60%	20.00%	$235	41.36%	$201	-$64	47.10%
1945	D	$223	$45	$93	($48)	1.40%	20.18%	$242	41.70%	$259	-$58	28.70%
1946	D	$222	$39	$55	($16)	-0.40%	17.57%	$224	24.77%	$269	-$11	4.20%
1947	D	$244	$39	$34	$5	9.90%	15.98%	$216	13.93%	$258	$11	-4.20%
1948	D	$269	$42	$30	$12	10.20%	15.61%	$214	11.15%	$252	$6	-2.30%
1949	D	$267	$39	$39	$0	-0.70%	14.61%	$219	14.61%	$253	-$1	0.20%
1950	D	$294	$39	$43	($4)	10.10%	13.27%	$214	14.63%	$257	-$5	1.80%
1951	D	$339	$52	$46	$6	15.30%	15.34%	$215	13.57%	$255	$2	-0.80%
1952	D	$358	$66	$68	($2)	5.60%	18.44%	$218	18.99%	$259	-$4	1.50%
1953	R	$379	$70	$76	($6)	5.90%	18.47%	$225	20.05%	$266	-$7	2.70%
1954	R	$380	$70	$71	($1)	0.30%	18.42%	$227	18.68%	$271	-$5	2.00%
1955	R	$415	$65	$68	($3)	9.20%	15.66%	$222	16.39%	$274	-$3	1.10%

(\$\$ in billions)

	President Party	GDP	Revenue	Outlay	Excess (deficit)	Change in GDP	Revenue % to GDP	Public Debt Outsdg	Outlay % to GDP	Federal Debt Outsdg	Federal Debt Change	Federal Debt % Change
1956	R	$437	$75	$71	$4	5.30%	17.16%	$219	16.25%	$273	$2	-0.60%
1957	R	$461	$80	$77	$3	5.50%	17.35%	$226	16.70%	$271	$2	-0.80%
1958	R	$467	$80	$82	($2)	1.30%	17.13%	$235	17.56%	$276	-$6	2.10%
1959	R	$507	$79	$92	($13)	8.60%	15.58%	$237	18.15%	$285	-$8	3.00%
1960	R	$526	$92	$92	$0	3.70%	17.49%	$238	17.49%	$286	-$2	0.60%
1961	R	$545	$94	$98	($4)	3.60%	17.25%	$248	17.98%	$289	-$3	0.90%
1962	D	$586	$100	$107	($7)	7.50%	17.06%	$254	18.26%	$298	-$9	3.20%
1963	D	$618	$107	$111	($4)	5.50%	17.31%	$257	17.96%	$306	-$8	2.50%
1964	D	$664	$113	$119	($6)	7.40%	17.02%	$261	17.92%	$312	-$6	1.90%
1965	D	$719	$117	$118	($1)	8.30%	16.27%	$264	16.41%	$317	-$6	1.80%
1966	D	$788	$131	$135	($4)	9.60%	16.62%	$267	17.13%	$320	-$3	0.90%
1967	D	$833	$149	$157	($8)	5.70%	17.89%	$290	18.85%	$326	-$6	2.00%
1968	D	$910	$153	$178	($25)	9.20%	16.81%	$278	19.56%	$348	-$21	6.50%
1969	D	$985	$187	$184	$3	8.20%	18.98%	$278	18.68%	$354	-$6	1.80%
1970	R	$1,039	$193	$196	($3)	5.50%	18.58%	$283	18.86%	$371	-$17	4.90%
1971	R	$1,127	$187	$210	($23)	8.50%	16.59%	$303	18.63%	$398	-$27	7.30%
1972	R	$1,238	$207	$231	($24)	9.80%	16.72%	$322	18.66%	$427	-$29	7.30%
1973	R	$1,383	$231	$246	($15)	11.70%	16.70%	$341	17.79%	$458	-$31	7.20%
1974	R	$1,500	$263	$269	($6)	8.50%	17.53%	$344	17.93%	$475	-$17	3.70%
1975	R	$1,638	$279	$332	($53)	9.20%	17.03%	$395	20.27%	$533	-$58	12.20%
1976	R	$1,825	$298	$371	($73)	11.40%	16.33%	$477	20.33%	$620	-$87	16.40%
1977	R	$2,031	$355	$409	($54)	11.30%	17.48%	$549	20.14%	$699	-$78	12.60%

(\$\$ in billions)	President Party	GDP	Revenue	Outlay	Excess (deficit)	Change in GDP	Revenue % to GDP	Public Debt Outsdg	Outlay % to GDP	Federal Debt Outsdg	Federal Debt Change	Federal Debt % Change
1978	D	\$2,298	\$400	\$459	(\$59)	13.10%	17.41%	\$607	19.97%	\$772	-\$73	10.40%
1979	D	\$2,563	\$463	\$504	(\$41)	11.50%	18.06%	\$640	19.66%	\$827	-\$55	7.10%
1980	D	\$2,790	\$517	\$591	(\$74)	8.90%	18.53%	\$712	21.18%	\$908	-\$81	9.80%
1981	D	\$3,129	\$599	\$678	(\$79)	12.20%	19.14%	\$789	21.67%	\$998	-\$90	9.90%
1982	R	\$3,255	\$617	\$745	(\$128)	4.00%	18.96%	\$924	22.89%	\$1,142	-\$144	14.50%
1983	R	\$3,537	\$600	\$808	(\$208)	8.70%	16.96%	\$1,137	22.84%	\$1,377	-\$235	20.60%
1984	R	\$3,933	\$667	\$852	(\$185)	11.20%	16.96%	\$1,307	21.66%	\$1,572	-\$195	14.20%
1985	R	\$4,220	\$734	\$946	(\$212)	7.30%	17.39%	\$1,507	22.42%	\$1,823	-\$251	16.00%
1986	R	\$4,463	\$769	\$990	(\$221)	5.80%	17.23%	\$1,741	22.18%	\$2,125	-\$302	16.60%
1987	R	\$4,740	\$854	\$1,004	(\$150)	6.20%	18.02%	\$1,890	21.18%	\$2,350	-\$225	10.60%
1988	R	\$5,104	\$909	\$1,065	(\$156)	7.70%	17.81%	\$2,052	20.87%	\$2,602	-\$252	10.70%
1989	R	\$5,884	\$991	\$1,144	(\$153)	15.30%	16.84%	\$2,191	19.44%	\$2,857	-\$255	9.80%
1990	R	\$5,803	\$1,032	\$1,253	(\$221)	-1.40%	17.78%	\$2,412	21.59%	\$3,233	-\$376	13.20%
1991	R	\$5,996	\$1,055	\$1,324	(\$269)	3.30%	17.60%	\$2,689	22.08%	\$3,665	-\$432	13.40%
1992	R	\$6,338	\$1,091	\$1,382	(\$291)	5.70%	17.21%	\$2,999	21.80%	\$4,065	-\$399	10.90%
1993	R	\$6,657	\$1,155	\$1,410	(\$255)	5.00%	17.35%	\$3,248	21.18%	\$4,411	-\$347	8.50%
1994	D	\$7,072	\$1,259	\$1,462	(\$203)	6.20%	17.80%	\$3,433	20.67%	\$4,693	-\$281	6.40%
1995	D	\$7,398	\$1,352	\$1,516	(\$164)	4.60%	18.28%	\$3,604	20.49%	\$4,974	-\$281	6.00%
1996	D	\$7,817	\$1,453	\$1,561	(\$108)	5.70%	18.59%	\$3,734	19.97%	\$5,225	-\$251	5.00%
1997	D	\$8,304	\$1,579	\$1,601	(\$22)	6.20%	19.01%	\$3,772	19.28%	\$5,413	-\$188	3.60%
1998	D	\$8,747	\$1,722	\$1,653	\$69	5.30%	19.69%	\$3,721	18.90%	\$5,526	-\$113	2.10%
1999	D	\$9,268	\$1,828	\$1,702	\$126	6.00%	19.72%	\$3,632	18.36%	\$5,656	-\$130	2.40%

(\$\$ in billions)

	President Party	GDP	Revenue	Outlay	Excess (deficit)	Change in GDP	Revenue % to GDP	Public Debt Outsdg	Outlay % to GDP	Federal Debt Outsdg	Federal Debt Change	Federal Debt % Change
2000	D	$9,817	$2,025	$1,789	$236	5.90%	20.63%	$3,410	18.22%	$5,674	-$18	0.30%
2001	D	$10,128	$1,991	$1,863	$128	3.20%	19.66%	$3,320	18.39%	$5,807	-$133	2.30%
2002	R	$10,470	$1,853	$2,011	($158)	3.40%	17.70%	$3,540	19.21%	$6,228	-$421	7.20%
2003	R	$10,961	$1,783	$2,160	($377)	4.70%	16.27%	$3,919	19.71%	$6,783	-$555	8.90%
2004	R	$11,686	$1,880	$2,293	($413)	6.60%	16.09%	$4,296	19.62%	$7,379	-$596	8.80%
2005	R	$12,422	$2,154	$2,472	($318)	6.30%	17.34%	$4,592	19.90%	$7,933	-$554	7.50%
2006	R	$13,178	$2,407	$2,655	($248)	6.10%	18.27%	$4,829	20.15%	$8,507	-$574	7.20%
2007	R	$13,808	$2,568	$2,729	($161)	4.80%	18.60%	$5,035	19.76%	$9,008	-$501	5.90%
2008	R	$14,265	$2,524	$2,982	($458)	3.30%	17.69%	$5,803	20.90%	$10,025	-$1,017	11.30%

APPENDIX B: WHO PAYS TAXES

2006 Adjusted Gross Income Level

		Under $50,000	$50,000 under $100,000	$100,000 under $200,000	$200,000 under $500,000	$500,000 under $1,000,000	$1,000,000 more
Returns in (000s)	92,741	47,845	28,799	12,041	3,115	588	353
% of total	100%	51.6%	31.1%	13.0%	3.4%	0.6%	0.4%
Net AGI (000,000s)	$7,439.5	$1,293.0	$2,044.9	$1,600.5	$893.3	$398.7	$1,209.0
% of total	100%	17.4%	27.5%	21.5%	12.0%	5.4%	16.3%
Taxes Paid (000,000s)	$1,023.9	$85.8	$184.4	$209.4	$177.0	$94.2	$273.1
% of total	100%	8.4%	18.0%	20.4%	17.3%	9.2%	26.7%
Tax % of AGI	13.8%	6.6%	9.0%	13.1%	19.8%	23.6%	22.6%

2005 Adjusted Gross Income Level

	Totals	Under $50,000	$50,000 under $100,000	$100,000 under $200,000	$200,000 under $500,000	$500,000 under $1,000,000	$1,000,000 more
Returns in (000s)	90,593	48,447	27,821	10,767	2,732	523	303
% of total	100%	53.5%	30.7%	11.9%	3.0%	0.6%	0.3%
Net AGI (000,000s)	$6,856.7	$1,299.0	$1,967.5	$1,425.1	$787.3	$354.5	$1,023.4
% of total	100%	18.9%	28.7%	20.8%	11.5%	5.2%	14.9%
Taxes Paid (000,000s)	$934.8	$86.8	$178.8	$189.5	$159.4	$84,700	$235.7
% of total	100%	9.3%	19.1%	20.3%	17.1%	9.1%	25.2%
Tax % of AGI	13.6%	6.7%	9.1%	13.3%	20.2%	23.9%	23.0%

APPENDIX C: SOCIAL SECURITY WAGE BASE AND TAX RATES

Year	Wage Base	Tax Rate	Taxes Generated
1963–65	$4,800	3.63%	$174
1966	$6,600	3.85%	$254
1967	$6,600	3.90%	$257
1968	$7,800	3.80%	$296
1969–70	$7,800	4.20%	$328
1971	$7,800	4.60%	$359
1972	$9,000	4.60%	$414
1973	$10,800	4.85%	$524
1974	$13,200	4.95%	$653
1975	$14,100	4.95%	$698
1976	$15,300	4.95%	$757
1977	$16,500	4.95%	$817
1978	$17,700	5.05%	$894
1979	$22,900	5.08%	$1,163
1980	$25,900	5.08%	$1,316
1981	$29,700	5.35%	$1,589
1982	$32,400	5.40%	$1,750
1983	$35,700	5.40%	$1,928
1984	$37,800	5.70%	$2,155
1985	$39,600	5.70%	$2,257
1986	$42,000	5.70%	$2,394
1987	$43,800	5.70%	$2,497
1988	$45,000	6.06%	$2,727
1989	$48,000	6.06%	$2,909
1990	$51,300	6.20%	$3,181
1991	$53,400	6.20%	$3,311
1992	$55,500	6.20%	$3,441
1993	$57,600	6.20%	$3,571
1994	$60,600	6.20%	$3,757
1995	$61,200	6.20%	$3,794
1996	$62,700	6.20%	$3,887
1997	$65,400	6.20%	$4,055
1998	$68,400	6.20%	$4,241
1999	$72,600	6.20%	$4,501
2000	$76,200	6.20%	$4,724
2001	$80,400	6.20%	$4,985
2002	$84,900	6.20%	$5,264
2003	$87,000	6.20%	$5,394
2004	$87,900	6.20%	$5,450
2005	$90,000	6.20%	$5,580
2006	$94,200	6.20%	$5,840
2007	$97,500	6.20%	$6,045

APPENDIX D: MEDICARE TAX BASE BY YEAR

Year	Wage Base	Combined Tax Rate
1966	$6,600	0.7%
1968	$7,800	1.2%
1972	$9,000	1.2%
1973	$10,800	2.0%
1974	$13,200	1.8%
1975	$14,100	1.8%
1976	$15,300	1.8%
1977	$16,500	1.8%
1978	$17,700	2.0%
1979	$22,900	2.1%
1980	$25,900	2.1%
1983	$35,700	2.6%
1984	$37,800	2.6%
1985	$39,600	2.7%
1986	$42,000	2.9%
1987	$43,800	2.9%
1988	$45,000	2.9%
1989	$48,000	2.9%
1990	$51,300	2.9%
1991	$125,000	2.9%
1992	$130,200	2.9%
1993	$135,000	2.9%
1993 and after	no limit	2.9%

NOTES

INTRODUCTION
President's Budget—Historical Tables
    http://www.whitehouse.gov/omb/budget/Historicals/
GAO-09-405SP Long-Term Fiscal Outlook March 2009
    http://www.gao.gov/new.items/d09405sp.pdf
Budget of the U.S. Government Fiscal Year 2011
    http://www.whitehouse.gov/omb/
Budget of the U.S. Government Fiscal Year 2010
    http://www.gpoaccess.gov/usbudget/fy10/browse.html
CIA World Factbook—Country Comparison—GDP (purchasing power parity)
    https://www.cia.gov/library/publications/the-world-factbook/rankorder/
    2001rank.html
The 2009 Annual Report of the Boards of Trustees of the Federal Hospital Insurance and Federal Supplementary Medical Insurance Trust Funds
    http://www.cms.gov/reportstrustfunds/downloads/tr2009.pdf

THE FINANCIAL TSUNAMI
President's Budget—Historical Tables
    http://www.whitehouse.gov/omb/budget/Historicals/

FUZZY MATH
President's Budget—Historical Tables
    http://www.whitehouse.gov/omb/budget/Historicals/
Budget of the U.S. Government Fiscal Year 2010
    http://www.gpoaccess.gov/usbudget/fy10/hist.html
Budget of the U.S. Government Fiscal Year 2011
    http://www.gpoaccess.gov/usbudget/fy11/hist.html
President's Budget—Historical Tables
    http://www.whitehouse.gov/omb/

Preliminary Analysis of the President's Budget and an Update of CBO's Budget and Economic Outlook

    http://www.cbo.gov/ftpdocs/100xx/doc10014/03-20-PresidentBudget.pdf

The Long-Term Budget Outlook

    http://www.cbo.gov/ftpdocs/69xx/doc6982/12-15-LongTermOutlook.pdf

FISCAL RESPONSIBILITY

President's Budget—Historical Tables

    http://www.whitehouse.gov/omb/budget/Historicals/

FISCAL RESPONSIBILITY WENT HAS DISAPPEARED

President's Budget—Historical Tables

    http://www.whitehouse.gov/omb/budget/Historicals/

Social Security Population and Dependency Ratios

    http://www.socialsecurity.gov/OACT/TR/2009/lr5a2.html

Mid-Session Review Budget of the U.S. Government FY 2010

    http://www.gpoaccess.gov/usbudget/fy10/pdf/10msr.pdf

The 2009 Annual Report of the Board of Trustees of the Federal Old-Age and Survivors Insurance and Federal Disability Insurance Trust Funds—Financial Outlook for Social Security—OASDI Trust Funds (4.A)

    https://www.socialsecurity.gov/policy/docs/statcomps/supplement/2009/4a.html

Social Security Online—The Official Web site of the U.S. Social Security Administration

    http://www.socialsecurity.gov/

Social Security Trustees Report Summary

    http://www.ssa.gov/OACT/TRSUM/index.html

Social Security Trust Fund Ratios

    http://www.ssa.gov/OACT/TR/2009/trLOF.html

Tax Data for Social Security & Medicare

    http://www.socialsecurity.gov/OACT/STATS/table3c3.html

Mid-Session Review Budget of the U.S. Government FY 2010

    http://www.gpoaccess.gov/usbudget/fy10/pdf/10msr.pdf

RECESSIONS ARE INEVITABLE

National Bureau of Economic Research

Hall, Robert (October 21, 2003). "The NBER's Recession Dating Procedure"

    http://www.nber.org/cycles/recessions.html

"The NBER's Recession Dating Procedure: Frequently Asked Questions"

    http://www.nber.org/cycles/recessions_faq.html

U.S. Business Cycle Expansions and Contractions, National Bureau of Economic Research.

    http://www.nber.org/cycles/cyclesmain.html

Stanley Lebergott (1957). "Annual Estimates of Unemployment in the United States, 1900–1954," *The Measurement and Behavior of Unemployment*
http://www.nber.org/chapters/c2644.pdf

Knoop, Todd A. (July 30, 2004). *Recessions and Depressions: Understanding Business Cycles*. Westport, CT, Praeger Publishers, 2004.

Goldberg, David J. (January 15, 1999). *Discontented America: The United States in the 1920s*. Baltimore, MD,The Johns Hopkins University Press 1999.

Vernon, J. R. (1991). "The 1920–21 Deflation: The Role of Aggregate Supply."
http://findarticles.com/p/articles/mi_hb5814/is_n3_v29/ai_n28604039/.

Kindleberger, Charles P. (1973). *The World in Depression, 1929–39*. Berkeley: University of California Press.

Labor Force Statistics from the Current Population Survey, Bureau of Labor Statistics. Labonte, Marc (January 10, 2002). "The Current Economic Recession." Congressional Research Service.
http://www.fpc.state.gov/documents/organization/7962.pdf

Carter, Susan B. (January 30, 2006). *The Historical Statistics of the United States*. Cambridge University Press.

Dell, S. (1957–06). "The United States Recession of 1953/54: A Comment." *The Economic Journal* 67 (266).

Merrill, Karen R. (2007). *The Oil Crisis of 1973–1974: A Brief History with Documents*. Bedford/St. Martin's.

CIA World Factbook—Country Comparison—Oil-consumption
https://www.cia.gov/library/publications/the-world-factbook/rankorder/2174rank.html

AFFORDABLE HOUSING AND THE HOUSING CRISIS

Budget of the U.S. Government Fiscal Year 2010
http://www.gpoaccess.gov/usbudget/fy10/browse.html

Government-Sponsored Enterprises (GSEs): An Institutional Overview
http://www.fas.org/sgp/crs/misc/RS21663.pdf

U.S. Department of Housing and Urban Development
Issue Brief: HUD's Affordable Lending Goals for Fannie Mae and Freddie Mac
http://www.huduser.org/portal/publications/polleg/gse.html

Census Bureau Home Page
http://www.census.gov/

U.S. Census Bureau—Financial Characteristics for Housing Units With a Mortgage
http://factfinder.census.gov/servlet/STTable?_bm=y&-geo_id=01000US&-qr_name=ACS_2008_3YR_G00_S2506&-ds_name=ACS_2008_3YR_G00_

Federal Funds Effective Rate
http://www.federalreserve.gov/releases/H15/data/Annual/H15_FF_O.txt

New Privately Owned Housing Units Started—Annual Data
http://www.census.gov/const/startsan.pdf

CASH FOR CLUNKERS

Cash for Clunkers Results Finally In: Taxpayers Paid $24,000 per Vehicle Sold, Reports Edmunds.com

http://www.edmunds.com/help/about/press/154387/article.html

THE EVOLUTION OF TAXES

Parkinson's Law

http://www.heretical.com/miscella/parkinsl.html

President's Budget—Historical Tables

Table 1.2—Summary of Receipts, Outlays, and Surpluses or Deficits (-) as Percentages of GDP: 1930–2015

http://www.whitehouse.gov/omb/budget/Historicals/

Table 1.1—Summary of Receipts, Outlays, and Surpluses or Deficits (-): 1789–2015

http://www.whitehouse.gov/omb/budget/Historicals/

SOURCES OF REVENUE

CBO—Revenues, Outlays, Surpluses, Deficits, and Debt Held by the Public, 1970 to 2009

http://www.cbo.gov/budget/historical.shtml

WHO PAYS AND HOW MUCH

Individual Income Tax Returns, 2007

http://www.irs.gov/pub/irs-soi/09fallbulindincomeret.pdf

Individual Income Tax Returns, 2007

http://www.irs.gov/pub/irs-soi/09winbulinincome.pdf

TAXES AND THE DEFICIT

Budget of the U.S. Government

http://www.gpoaccess.gov/usbudget/

Bureau of Labor Statistics Data

U.S. Budget Historical Tables

http://www.gpoaccess.gov/usbudget/fy09/hist.html

http://www.gpoaccess.gov/usbudget/fy10/hist.html

http://www.gpoaccess.gov/usbudget/fy11/hist.html

47% of households owe no tax—and their ranks are growing (Sep. 30, 2009)

http://money.cnn.com/2009/09/30/pf/taxes/who_pays_taxes/index.htm

Office of Tax Analysis—Revenue Effects of Major tax Bills

http://www.ustreas.gov/offices/tax-policy/library/ota81.pdf

CA 2009–10 Budget Analysis Series; The Fiscal Outlook Under the February Budget Package

http://www.lao.ca.gov/LAOApp/PubDetails.aspx?id=1967

CBO Budget and Economic Outlook Fiscal Years 2010 to 2020
  http://www.cbo.gov/ftpdocs/108xx/doc10871/Frontmatter.shtml
Gallop—Views of Income Taxes Among Most Positive Since 1956 (April 13, 2009)
  http://www.gallup.com/poll/117433/views-income-taxes-among-positive-1956.aspx
Cost of the Wars
  http://www.csbaonline.org/4Publications/PubLibrary/R.20081215.Cost_of_the_Wars_i/R.20081215.Cost_of_the_Wars_i.pdf
Congressional Research Service
The Cost of Iraq, Afghanistan, and Other Global War on Terror Operations Since 9/11
  http://assets.opencrs.com/rpts/RL33110_20090928.pdf
Individual Income Tax Returns, 2007
  http://www.irs.gov/pub/irs-soi/09fallbulindincomeret.pdf

OUTLAYS AND THEIR IMPACT ON THE NATIONAL DEBT

President's Budget—Historical Tables
Table 1.1—Summary of Receipts, Outlays, and Surpluses or Deficits (–): 1789–2015
  http://www.whitehouse.gov/omb/budget/Historicals/
Budget of the U.S. Government Fiscal Year 2011
  http://www.whitehouse.gov/omb/
Treasury Direct
  http://www.treasurydirect.gov/
Treasury Direct—Debt to the Penny (Daily History Search Application)
  http://www.treasurydirect.gov/NP/NPGateway
Federal Revenue and Spending Budget Chart Book Federal Spending—By the Numbers
  http://www.heritage.org/budgetchartbook/

A NEED FOR BALANCE AND PRIORITY

President's Budget—Historical Tables
  http://www.whitehouse.gov/omb/budget/Historicals/
Table 1.1— Summary of Receipts, Outlays, and Surpluses or Deficits (–): 1789–2015
  http://www.whitehouse.gov/omb/budget/Historicals/
GAO Financial Audit—Bureau of the Public Debt's Fiscal Years 2009 and 2008 Schedules of Federal Debt
  http://www.treasurydirect.gov/govt/reports/pd/feddebt/feddebt_ann2009.pdf
Social Security Trustees Report Summary
  http://www.ssa.gov/OACT/TRSUM/index.html

ON-BUDGET/OFF-BUDGET DEFICITS AND SURPLUSES

Treasury Direct
  http://www.treasurydirect.gov/

Budget of the U.S. Government Fiscal Year 2011—Table S-3
http://www.whitehouse.gov/omb/
Budget of the U.S. Government Fiscal Year 2010—Table S-3
http://www.gpoaccess.gov/usbudget/fy10/browse.html

INTERGOVERNMENTAL DEBT IS REALLY PUBLIC DEBT
Social Security Trustees Report Summary
http://www.ssa.gov/OACT/TRSUM/index.html
President's Budget—Historical Tables
http://www.whitehouse.gov/omb/budget/Historicals/
Table 1.1— Summary of Receipts, Outlays, and Surpluses or Deficits (-): 1789–2015
http://www.whitehouse.gov/omb/budget/Historicals/

WHERE DOES THE MONEY GO?
CBO——Revenues, Outlays, Surpluses, Deficits, and Debt Held by the Public,
1970 to 2009, Table F.5
http://www.cbo.gov/budget/historical.shtml
Budget of the U.S. Government Fiscal Year 2011
http://www.whitehouse.gov/omb/
Treasury Direct
http://www.treasurydirect.gov/govt/reports/ir/ir_expense.htm

SOCIAL SECURITY TRUST FUND
Social Security Trustees Report Summary
http://www.ssa.gov/OACT/TRSUM/index.html
Social Security—A Brief History
http://www.socialsecurity.gov/history/pdf/2007historybooklet.pdf
The 2007 Annual Report of the Boards of Trustees of the Federal Old-Age and
Survivors Insurance and Federal Disability Insurance Trust Funds Table IV.B2
http://www.ssa.gov/OACT/TR/TR07/tr07.pdf
The 2007 Annual Report of the Boards of Trustees of the Federal Old-Age and
Survivors Insurance and Federal Disability Insurance Trust Funds Table IV.B2
http://www.ssa.gov/OACT/TR/TR09/tr09.pdf
Budget of the U.S. Government: Fiscal Year 2009
http://www.gpoaccess.gov/usbudget/fy09/browse.html

MEDICARE
Table VI.F2.—OASDI and HI Annual Income Rates, Cost Rates, and Balances,
Calendar Years 2009–85
[As a percentage of taxable payroll]
http://www.ssa.gov/OACT/TR/2009/VI_OASDHI_payroll.html#134104

Social Security & Medicare Tax Rates
   http://www.ssa.gov/OACT/ProgData/taxRates.html
   http://www.ssa.gov/OACT/COLA/cbb.html#Series
President's Budget—Historical Tables
   http://www.whitehouse.gov/omb/budget/Historicals/